most loved recipe collection most loved recipe collection most loved recipe collection
most loved recipe collection most loved recipe collection most loved recipe collection
most loved recipe collection most loved recipe collection most loved recipe collection
most loved recipe collection most loved recipe collection most loved recipe collection
most loved recipe collection most loved recipe collection most loved recipe collection
most loved recipe collection most loved recipe collection most loved recipe collection

most loved recipe collection most loved recipe collection most loved recipe collection
most loved recipe collection most loved recipe collection most loved recipe collection
most loved recipe collection most loved recipe collection most loved recipe collection
most loved recipe collection most loved recipe collection most loved recipe collection
most loved recipe collection most loved recipe collection most loved recipe collection
most loved recipe collection most loved recipe collection most loved recipe collection
most loved recipe collection most loved recipe collection most loved recipe collection
most loved recipe collection most loved recipe collection most loved recipe collection
most loved recipe collection most loved recipe collection most loved recipe collection
most loved recipe collection most loved recipe collection most loved recipe collection
most loved recipe collection most loved recipe collection most loved recipe collection
most loved recipe collection most loved recipe collection most loved recipe collection
most loved recipe collection most loved recipe collection most loved recipe collection
most loved recipe collection most loved recipe collection most loved recipe collection
most loved recipe collection most loved recipe collection most loved recipe collection
most loved recipe collection most loved recipe collection most loved recipe collection
most loved recipe collection most loved recipe collection most loved recipe collection
most loved recipe collection most loved recipe collection most loved recipe collection
most loved recipe collection most loved recipe collection most loved recipe collection
most loved recipe collection most loved recipe collection most loved recipe

most
loved

Pictured on front cover:
Easy Stir-Fry, page 54

Pictured on back cover:
1. Shrimp And Pea Stir-Fry, page 81
2. Cashew Vegetable Stir-Fry, page 110

First Printing April 2007

Library and Archives Canada Cataloguing in Publication
Paré, Jean, date
Most loved stir-fries / by Jean Paré.
(Most loved recipe collection)
Includes index.
ISBN 978-1-897069-16-5
1. Stir frying. 2. Wok cookery. I. Title. II. Series: Paré, Jean, date- .
Most loved recipe collection.
TX689.5.P36 2007   641.7'7   C2006-904816-9

Published by
Company's Coming Publishing Limited
2311 – 96 Street
Edmonton, Alberta, Canada T6N 1G3
Tel: 780-450-6223   Fax: 780-450-1857
www.companyscoming.com

Company's Coming is a registered trademark owned by
Company's Coming Publishing Limited

Printed in China

We gratefully acknowledge the following suppliers for their generous support of our Test and Photography Kitchens:

Broil King Barbecues
Corelle®
Hamilton Beach® Canada
Lagostina®
Proctor Silex® Canada
Tupperware®

Our special thanks to the following businesses for providing props for photography:

Artifacts
Casa Bugatti
Cherison Enterprises Inc.
Chintz & Company
Danesco Inc.
Dansk Gifts
La Cache
Le Gnome
Linens 'N Things
Mikasa Home Store
Out of the Fire Studio
Pfaltzgraff Canada
Pier 1 Imports
Salisbury Greenhouse
Stokes
The Bay
Totally Bamboo
X/S Wares
Winners Stores

Pictured from left: Sweet-And-Sour Pork, page 100; Asian Citrus Chicken, page 56; Bibimbap, page 12; Broccoli Shrimp Stir-Fry, page 66

table of contents

the Company's Coming story

"never share a recipe you wouldn't use yourself"

Jean Paré (pronounced "jeen PAIR-ee") grew up understanding that the combination of family, friends and home cooking is the best recipe for a good life. From her mother, she learned to appreciate good cooking, while her father praised even her earliest attempts in the kitchen. When Jean left home, she took with her a love of cooking, many family recipes and an intriguing desire to read cookbooks as if they were novels!

In 1963, when her four children had all reached school age, Jean volunteered to cater the 50th Anniversary of the Vermilion School of Agriculture, now Lakeland College, in Alberta, Canada. Working out of her home, Jean prepared a dinner for more than 1,000 people, which launched a flourishing catering operation that continued for over 18 years. During that time, she had countless opportunities to test new ideas with immediate feedback—resulting in empty plates and contented customers! Whether preparing cocktail sandwiches for a house party or serving a hot meal for 1,500 people, Jean Paré earned a reputation for good food, courteous service and reasonable prices.

As requests for her recipes mounted, Jean was often asked the question, "Why don't you write a cookbook?" Jean responded by teaming up with her son, Grant Lovig, in the fall of 1980 to form Company's Coming Publishing Limited. The publication of *150 Delicious Squares* on April 14, 1981 marked the debut of what would soon become one of the world's most popular cookbook series.

The company has grown since those early days when Jean worked from a spare bedroom in her home. Today, she continues to write recipes while working closely with the staff of the Recipe Factory, as the Company's Coming test kitchen is affectionately known. There she fills the role of mentor, assisting with the development of recipes people most want to use for everyday cooking and easy entertaining. Every Company's Coming recipe is *kitchen-tested* before it's approved for publication.

Jean's daughter, Gail Lovig, is responsible for marketing and distribution, leading a team that includes sales personnel located in major cities across Canada. In addition, Company's Coming cookbooks are published and distributed under licence in the United States, Australia and other world markets. Bestsellers many times over in English, Company's Coming cookbooks have also been published in French and Spanish.

Familiar and trusted in home kitchens around the world, Company's Coming cookbooks are offered in a variety of formats. Highly regarded as kitchen workbooks, the softcover Original Series, with its lay-flat plastic comb binding, is still a favourite among readers.

Jean Paré's approach to cooking has always called for *quick and easy recipes* using *everyday ingredients*. That view has served her well. The recipient of many awards, including the Queen Elizabeth Golden Jubilee medal, Jean was appointed a Member of the Order of Canada, her country's highest lifetime achievement honour.

Jean continues to gain new supporters by adhering to what she calls The Golden Rule of Cooking: *"Never share a recipe you wouldn't use yourself."* It's an approach that works—*millions of times over!*

foreword

Imagine a medley of fresh vegetables made more brilliant by a quick pass across a pan, then nestled into a bed of rice or pasta to highlight the contrast in colours. A properly-cooked stir-fry is a feast for the eyes—little wonder that these gorgeous dishes have shown up at feasts and banquets around the world as a delectable display of the local fare.

But visual appeal is just a small part of the stir-fry's claim to fame. These are dishes developed in countries where heating fuel is hard to come by, so meals must be cooked quickly. By chopping vegetables and meat into uniform, bite-sized pieces, ingredients can be rapidly heated in little fat and flavoured with interesting spices or sauces. Whether you're a street vendor in Mexico or Malaysia with just a small bottle of propane, or a North American parent trying to get the kids to soccer practice on time, this speedy cooking style makes sense. It's fast food that tastes fabulous!

Most Loved Stir-Fries offers everything you need to know about these wonderful dishes. Collected from the Company's Coming's library, these favourites of staff and loyal readers reflect the tastes of our far-flung world. From a French Beef Bourguignon (after all, they introduced the term *sauté* to the English language!) to Chinese Five-Spice Shrimp, it's all here, complete with notes and tips about international ingredients, substitutions and serving suggestions. And while a wok is nice to have, your cooking will still be a success using a basic frying pan—in fact, it is suggested as a first choice in some of our recipes.

Many of our stir-fries call for fresh vegetables (such a simple way to boost your family's fruit-and-veggie servings), but we've also included meals that call for frozen ingredients and instant rice when you're in a rush. Always make sure that you have all your ingredients cut and ready before you start cooking—we did say it was a fast-cooking method! And keep in mind that most vegetables can be prepared ahead of time, so if you're already chopping up half an onion, for instance, do the other half and refrigerate it in an airtight container for tomorrow's dinner.

Or get family and friends slicing and dicing while you catch up on the day. With home cooking this easy, you'll want *Most Loved Stir-Fries* in your kitchen tonight!

Jean Paré

nutrition information

Each recipe is analyzed using the most current version of the Canadian Nutrient File from Health Canada—which is based on the United States Department of Agriculture (USDA) Nutrient Database.

- If more than one ingredient is listed (such as "hard margarine or butter"), or if a range is given (1 – 2 tsp., 5 – 10 mL), only the first ingredient or first amount is analyzed.

- For meat, poultry and fish, the serving size per person is based on the recommended 4 oz. (113 g) uncooked weight (without bone), which is 2 – 3 oz. (57 – 85 g) cooked weight (without bone)—approximately the size of a deck of playing cards.

- Milk used is 1% M.F. (milk fat), unless otherwise stated.

- Cooking oil used is canola oil, unless otherwise stated.

- Ingredients indicating "sprinkle," "optional," or "for garnish" are not included in the nutrition information.

- The fat in recipes and combination foods can vary greatly depending on the sources and types of fats used in each specific ingredient. For these reasons, the amount of saturated, monounsaturated and polyunsaturated fats may not add up to the total fat content.

Vera C. Mazurak, Ph.D.
Nutritionist

Cash in on the pleasing taste of cashews in this delightfully textured crowd-pleaser! Best served over steamed rice.

about choosing woks

Although a large frying pan will do in a pinch, woks are made for stir-frying. The best material for a wok is carbon steel because it is inexpensive and not too heavy. Although many woks are made with non-stick coating, this is not necessary for stir-frying. As long as the wok has been properly seasoned and heated to a high enough temperature, you shouldn't have a problem with food sticking. Woks are sold with 2 small handles or 1 long one. If you have weaker wrists, you'll want to opt for the two-handle version.

Tender Beef And Cashews

Soy sauce	1 tbsp.	15 mL
Dry sherry	2 tsp.	10 mL
Garlic clove, minced (or 1/4 tsp., 1 mL, powder)	1	1
Sesame oil	1/2 tsp.	2 mL
Granulated sugar	1/2 tsp.	2 mL
Pepper, sprinkle		
Beef tenderloin steak (3/4 inch, 2 cm, thick), cut in half lengthwise and cut across grain into 1/8 inch (3 mm) thick slices	3/4 lb.	340 g
Water	1/4 cup	60 mL
Cornstarch	1 tbsp.	15 mL
Oyster sauce	2 tbsp.	30 mL
Peanut (or cooking) oil	1 tbsp.	15 mL
Green onions, cut into 1 inch (2.5 cm) pieces	3	3
Peanut (or cooking) oil	1 tbsp.	15 mL
Can of whole baby corn, drained and cut in half lengthwise	14 oz.	398 mL
Can of sliced water chestnuts, drained	8 oz.	227 mL
Sliced celery	1/2 cup	125 mL
Sliced red pepper	1/2 cup	125 mL
Thinly sliced carrot	1/3 cup	75 mL
Raw cashews, toasted (see Tip, page 56)	2/3 cup	150 mL

Combine first 6 ingredients in medium bowl.

Add beef. Stir. Let stand at room temperature for 10 minutes, stirring occasionally.

Stir water into cornstarch in small cup. Add oyster sauce. Stir. Set aside.

Heat wok or large frying pan on medium-high until very hot. Add first amount of peanut oil. Add beef mixture and green onion. Stir-fry for 3 to 4 minutes until beef reaches desired doneness. Transfer to small bowl. Cover to keep warm.

(continued on next page)

Add second amount of peanut oil to hot wok. Add next 5 ingredients. Stir-fry for 2 to 3 minutes until vegetables are tender-crisp.

Add beef mixture and cashews. Stir cornstarch mixture. Add to beef mixture. Heat and stir for 2 to 3 minutes until boiling and thickened. Serves 4.

1 serving: 625 Calories; 38.6 g Total Fat (18.1 g Mono, 5.5 g Poly, 11.6 g Sat); 73 mg Cholesterol; 45 g Carbohydrate; 6 g Fibre; 29 g Protein; 480 mg Sodium

Pictured below.

For those about to wok, we salute you with this quick and easy fresh-tasting stir-fry. Serve over hot noodles and add a slice of garlic toast.

how to season a wok

All new cast iron woks (and cast iron frying pans, for that matter) should be seasoned before using. It's a simple procedure and, if done a couple times a year, should give your cookware a natural non-stick surface. Simply pour canola oil on a paper towel and grease the interior of the wok. Heat the wok on a low temperature for about five minutes. Allow to cool, then wipe off the oil with a clean paper towel. Repeat this procedure a few more times until your wok has a well-oiled shine.

Beef And Zucchini

Water	1/4 cup	60 mL
Cornstarch	2 tsp.	10 mL
White vinegar	1 tbsp.	15 mL
Granulated sugar	1/2 tsp.	2 mL
Garlic salt	1/4 tsp.	1 mL
Onion salt	1/8 tsp.	0.5 mL
Dried oregano	1/8 tsp.	0.5 mL
Ground thyme, just a pinch		
Olive (or cooking) oil	1 tbsp.	15 mL
Beef top sirloin steak, cut into 1/8 inch (3 mm) thick strips	3/4 lb.	340 g
Salt, sprinkle		
Pepper, sprinkle		
Olive (or cooking) oil	1 tsp.	5 mL
Medium zucchini, thinly sliced	1	1
Cherry tomatoes, halved	1 cup	250 mL

Grated Parmesan cheese, sprinkle (optional)

Stir water into cornstarch in small bowl. Add next 6 ingredients. Stir. Set aside.

Heat wok or large frying pan on medium-high until very hot. Add first amount of olive oil. Add beef. Stir-fry for 3 to 4 minutes until beef reaches desired doneness. Sprinkle with salt and pepper. Transfer to separate small bowl. Cover to keep warm.

Add second amount of olive oil to hot wok. Add zucchini. Stir-fry for 2 to 3 minutes until tender-crisp.

Add beef and tomato. Stir cornstarch mixture. Add to beef mixture. Heat and stir for 2 to 3 minutes until boiling and thickened.

Sprinkle with Parmesan cheese. Serves 4.

1 serving: 256 Calories; 17.5 g Total Fat (8.8 g Mono, 1.0 g Poly, 5.8 g Sat); 47 mg Cholesterol; 6 g Carbohydrate; 1 g Fibre; 19 g Protein; 120 mg Sodium

Pictured at right.

Curry makes fruit for dinner a most natural choice. When spicy curry melds with sweet fruit, it's undeniable—the two go together like sun and shine! Serve over rice or couscous for a complete meal.

about fruits and vegetables

So, exactly how many servings of fruits and vegetables is a person supposed to eat each day? With Health Canada's recommended allowance of 5 to 10 servings per day, the thought of having to eat that much produce may appear quite daunting. Fear not. First, the number of recommended servings will vary based on a person's age, size and activity level. For example a child or smaller person who does not exercise very much should aim for 5 servings a day, whereas a larger person who exercises extensively will need more fuel and should aim for 10. Second, serving sizes are actually a lot smaller than many people think. A serving can consist of 1 medium-sized fruit or vegetable, 1/2 cup (125 mL) fresh, frozen or canned vegetables, 1 cup (250 mL) salad or 1/2 cup (125 mL) juice. Keeping this in mind, a plate of stir-fried veggies may contain 2 or 3 servings.

Fruity Beef Curry

Cooking oil	2 tsp.	10 mL
Lean ground beef	1 lb.	454 g
Salt	1 tsp.	5 mL
Chopped onion	1 1/2 cups	375 mL
Cumin seed	1 tbsp.	15 mL
Coarsely grated gingerroot (or 1/2 tsp., 2 mL, ground ginger)	2 tsp.	10 mL
Turmeric	1 tsp.	5 mL
Ground cardamom	1/2 tsp.	2 mL
Bay leaf	1	1
Ground cloves	1/8 tsp.	0.5 mL
Dried crushed chilies (optional)	1/2 tsp.	2 mL
Medium tomatoes, seeds removed, chopped	3	3
Medium cooking apples (such as McIntosh), peeled and cut into 6 wedges each	2	2
Sultana raisins	1/2 cup	125 mL
Grated zest and juice of 1 medium lemon		
Medium bananas, cut into 1 inch (2.5 cm) pieces	2	2
Chopped ripe mango	1 cup	250 mL
Liquid honey	2 tbsp.	30 mL
Unsalted cashews	1/3 cup	75 mL

Heat cooking oil in large frying pan on medium. Add beef and salt. Stir-fry for about 10 minutes until beef is no longer pink. Drain.

Add next 8 ingredients. Stir. Cook for 5 to 10 minutes, stirring often, until onion is softened.

Add next 4 ingredients, reserving half of lemon zest. Stir. Cook, covered, for about 5 minutes, stirring occasionally, until apple starts to soften.

Add next 3 ingredients. Stir. Cook, covered, for 1 to 2 minutes until heated through and fruit is slightly softened. Discard bay leaf.

Sprinkle individual servings with cashews and reserved lemon zest. Serves 4.

1 serving: 605 Calories; 24.8 g Total Fat (11.9 g Mono, 2.4 g Poly, 7.8 g Sat); 68 mg Cholesterol; 75 g Carbohydrate; 8 g Fibre; 27 g Protein; 676 mg Sodium

Pictured at right.

As fast as you can say BIH-bim-bap, this Korean vegetable and beef rice bowl can be on the table. The beef is slightly sweet and the vegetables are crisp and flavourful.

about daikon radish

The word daikon is derived from the Japanese words *dai*, meaning large, and *kon*, meaning root. It has a crisp, juicy white flesh and a slightly sweet, mild flavour. It also goes by the names *mooli*, winter radish, Japanese radish and Chinese radish. When shopping for this unusual vegetable, choose specimens that are firm and unwrinkled with a somewhat shiny surface, rather than a matte one. Store in the refrigerator, wrapped in plastic, for up to 1 week, and always peel before using.

Bibimbap

Beef top sirloin steak	1/2 lb.	225 g
Soy sauce	2 tbsp.	30 mL
Sesame (or cooking) oil	1 tbsp.	15 mL
Liquid honey	2 tsp.	10 mL
Dry sherry	2 tsp.	10 mL
Hot cooked long grain white rice (about 1 1/3 cups, 325 mL, uncooked)	4 cups	1 L
Cooking oil	2 tsp.	10 mL
Medium carrot, very thinly sliced	1	1
Julienned peeled daikon radish (see Tip, page 110)	1/2 cup	125 mL
Salt	1/4 tsp.	1 mL
Pepper, sprinkle		
Cayenne pepper, sprinkle		
Fresh bean sprouts	1 1/2 cups	375 mL
Chopped fresh spinach leaves, lightly packed	1 cup	250 mL

Cut steak across grain into 1/4 x 2 inch (0.6 x 5 cm) slices. Cut slices lengthwise into 1/4 inch (6 mm) strips.

Combine next 4 ingredients in medium bowl. Add beef. Stir. Let stand at room temperature for 15 minutes, stirring occasionally. Heat wok or large frying pan on medium-high until very hot. Add beef mixture. Stir-fry for about 2 minutes until beef reaches desired doneness.

Spoon rice into 4 individual serving bowls. Spoon beef mixture over rice. Cover to keep warm.

Add cooking oil to hot wok. Add next 5 ingredients. Stir-fry for 1 to 2 minutes until carrot is tender-crisp.

Add bean sprouts and spinach. Stir-fry for about 1 minute until spinach is wilted. Spoon vegetable mixture over beef. Serves 4.

1 serving: 443 Calories; 14.8 g Total Fat (6.2 g Mono, 2.5 g Poly, 3.9 g Sat); 42 mg Cholesterol; 54 g Carbohydrate; 2 g Fibre; 22 g Protein; 830 mg Sodium

Pictured at right.

Serve with fresh, thin Chinese-style egg noodles to soak up the thick, rich sauce.

how to use chopsticks

1. Place upper portion of 1 chopstick in curve between thumb and first finger (index finger) of your dominant eating hand, resting lower portion against side of fourth (ring) finger in a stationary position. You should not be able to wiggle this chopstick.

2. Place upper portion of second chopstick above first chopstick, between tip of thumb and side of first finger and resting against middle finger (similar to how you might hold a pen or pencil). You should be able to wiggle this chopstick.

3. By moving your index finger, move the top chopstick up and down, creating an open and close action against the bottom chopstick, perfect for picking up everything from dim sum dumplings to pea pods.

Saucy Ginger Beef

Low-sodium soy sauce	3 tbsp.	50 mL
Cornstarch	1 tbsp.	15 mL
Dry sherry	1 tbsp.	15 mL
Garlic clove, minced (or 1/4 tsp., 1 mL, powder)	1	1
Granulated sugar	1 tsp.	5 mL
Dried crushed chilies	1/4 tsp.	1 mL
Ground ginger	1/4 tsp.	1 mL
Salt	1/4 tsp.	1 mL
Beef top sirloin steak, cut into 1/8 inch (3 mm) thick strips	3/4 lb.	340 g
Water	3/4 cup	175 mL
Cornstarch	1 tbsp.	15 mL
Cooking oil	1 tsp.	5 mL
Large onion, sliced	1	
Granulated sugar	1 tsp.	5 mL
Cooking oil	1 tbsp.	15 mL

Sliced green onion, for garnish

Stir soy sauce into first amount of cornstarch in medium bowl. Add next 6 ingredients. Stir.

Add beef. Stir. Cover. Let stand in refrigerator for 30 minutes, stirring occasionally.

Stir water into second amount of cornstarch in small cup. Set aside.

Heat wok or large frying pan on medium-high until very hot. Add first amount of cooking oil. Add onion. Stir-fry for 5 to 6 minutes until onion is softened.

Sprinkle with sugar. Stir-fry for 5 to 6 minutes until onion is golden.

Add second amount of cooking oil to onion. Transfer beef to hot wok with slotted spoon, reserving soy sauce mixture. Stir-fry for 2 to 3 minutes until beef reaches desired doneness. Add soy sauce mixture. Stir cornstarch mixture. Add to beef mixture. Heat and stir for 2 to 3 minutes until boiling and thickened.

(continued on next page)

Garnish with green onion. Serves 4.

1 serving: 315 Calories; 16.7 g Total Fat (7.7 g Mono, 1.9 g Poly, 5.1 g Sat); 64 mg Cholesterol;
16 g Carbohydrate; 1 g Fibre; 24 g Protein; 532 mg Sodium

Pictured below.

Top: Saucy Ginger Beef, page 14
Bottom: Ginger Beef, page 16

No need to slice up the beef—this fast and easy recipe uses ground beef to cut down on the prep time. Delicious over fresh, thin Chinese-style egg noodles.

about gingerroot

Ginger is used fresh in a wide variety of Asian and Indian cuisines, where it adds its distinct zing to stir fries, soups, marinades and almost anything else you can imagine. In the western world, dried ginger has traditionally been more popular than fresh and is used to spice up sweet foods, especially baked goods like the ever-popular gingerbread. Although the two versions are essentially the same thing, the processing has made their flavours different—so it is inadvisable to use them interchangeably in a recipe, unless you are given that option. But you can certainly justify buying the fresh root because, if stored properly, it can last 3 weeks in the refrigerator and up to 6 months in the freezer. To freeze, just wrap the unpeeled root tightly in plastic before putting it in the freezer. When it is needed, cut off the quantity you are going to use and put the rest back in the freezer.

Ginger Beef

Water	2/3 cup	150 mL
Oyster sauce	1/4 cup	60 mL
Granulated sugar	1 tbsp.	15 mL
Cornstarch	2 tsp.	10 mL
Beef bouillon powder	1 tsp.	5 mL
Sesame oil	1 tsp.	5 mL
Dried crushed chilies	1/2 tsp.	2 mL
Cornstarch	2 tbsp.	30 mL
Soy sauce	1 tbsp.	15 mL
Finely grated gingerroot	2 tsp.	10 mL
Garlic clove, minced (or 1/4 tsp., 1 mL, powder)	1	1
Onion powder	1/4 tsp.	1 mL
Extra-lean ground beef	1 lb.	454 g
Cooking oil	1 tbsp.	15 mL
Thinly sliced green pepper	1 cup	250 mL
Green onions, cut into 1/2 inch (12 mm) pieces	6	6

Combine first 7 ingredients in small bowl. Set aside.

Combine next 5 ingredients in medium bowl.

Add beef. Mix well.

Heat cooking oil in large frying pan on medium. Add beef mixture. Stir. Cook for about 10 minutes, coarsely breaking up beef, until no longer pink. Drain.

Add green pepper and green onion. Heat and stir for 2 minutes. Stir oyster sauce mixture. Add to beef mixture. Heat and stir for about 1 minute until boiling and thickened. Serves 4.

1 serving: 270 Calories; 13.3 g Total Fat (6.2 g Mono, 1.8 g Poly, 4.0 g Sat); 62 mg Cholesterol; 12 g Carbohydrate; 1 g Fibre; 25 g Protein; 522 mg Sodium

Pictured on page 15.

Beef In Black Bean Sauce

Egg white (large), fork-beaten	1	1
Dry sherry	2 tbsp.	30 mL
Oyster sauce	1 tbsp.	15 mL
Concentrated black bean sauce	1 tbsp.	15 mL
Garlic cloves, minced (or 1/2 tsp., 2 mL, powder)	2	2
Granulated sugar	1 tsp.	5 mL
Beef tenderloin steak, cut into 1/8 inch (3 mm) thick slices	1 lb.	454 g
Water	1 tsp.	5 mL
Cornstarch	1 tsp.	5 mL
Cooking oil	1 1/2 tbsp.	25 mL
Green onions, cut into 1 inch (2.5 cm) pieces	8	8

Combine first 6 ingredients in medium bowl.

Add beef. Stir. Let stand at room temperature for up to 30 minutes, stirring occasionally.

Stir water into cornstarch in small cup. Set aside.

Heat wok or large frying pan on medium-high until very hot. Add cooking oil. Add beef mixture. Stir-fry for 3 to 4 minutes until beef reaches desired doneness.

Stir cornstarch mixture. Add to beef mixture. Add green onion. Heat and stir until boiling and thickened. Serves 4.

1 serving: 373 Calories; 24.8 g Total Fat (11.2 g Mono, 2.3 g Poly, 8.1 g Sat); 102 mg Cholesterol; 4 g Carbohydrate; 1 g Fibre; 31 g Protein; 132 mg Sodium

Bring out the big guns, this dish calls for the heavy artillery! To experience the full-flavour explosion, make sure you are using the thick, chunky, concentrated bean sauce that comes in a jar. Serve with rice.

about black bean sauce

When purchasing black bean sauce, it is important to note that there are two very different products with the same name. The concentrated sauce is thick, chunky and has pieces of fermented soybeans in it. It should be used only in small amounts because of its strong flavour. The other sauce (what we refer to as pourable black bean sauce in our recipes) is thinner, smoother and has water as the first ingredient. It can be used as is from the bottle without overpowering other ingredients in your dishes.

Thai cooking is known for showcasing a variety of flavours and colours in its fresh cuisine—and this dish certainly keeps up with tradition! Peanut sauce adds nice flavour and can be found in the Asian section of your grocery store.

In mid-April, the Songkran Festival takes place in Thailand. Celebrating movement, festival revelers often splash water on one another. Celebrate in your own style with a delicious Thai-inspired menu (water splashing optional). Start with fried wontons or Thai-flavoured chicken wings from your grocer's freezer. Serve Thai Noodles as your main course and complete your feast with chocolate dipped banana slices for dessert! Decorate your table with Thai silk cloth and, as a centrepiece, float a few lotus blossoms (or your favourite flower) in a large, shallow bowl of water.

Thai Noodles

Broken up fettuccine noodles	4 cups	1 L
Cooking oil	1 tsp.	5 mL
Lean ground beef	1 lb.	454 g
Sesame (or cooking) oil	2 tsp.	10 mL
Medium red pepper, thinly sliced	1	1
Medium yellow pepper, thinly sliced	1	1
Chopped onion	1 cup	250 mL
Garlic cloves, minced (or 3/4 tsp., 4 mL, powder)	3	3
Finely grated gingerroot (or 1/4 tsp., 1 mL, ground ginger)	1 1/2 tsp.	7 mL
Dried crushed chilies	1/4 tsp.	1 mL
Can of stewed tomatoes, broken up	14 oz.	398 mL
Low-sodium soy sauce	3 tbsp.	50 mL
Peanut sauce	2 tbsp.	30 mL
Granulated sugar	1 tsp.	5 mL
Red wine vinegar	1 tsp.	5 mL
Ground coriander	1 tsp.	5 mL
Salt	1/2 tsp.	2 mL
Pepper	1/4 tsp.	1 mL

Cook fettuccine in boiling salted water in large uncovered saucepan or Dutch oven for 5 to 7 minutes, stirring occasionally, until tender but firm. Drain. Return to same pot. Cover to keep warm.

Heat wok or large frying pan on medium. Add cooking oil. Add beef. Stir-fry for about 10 minutes until no longer pink. Drain. Transfer to small bowl. Cover to keep warm.

Add sesame oil to hot wok. Add next 6 ingredients. Stir-fry for 3 to 5 minutes until onion is softened.

Add remaining 8 ingredients and beef. Stir. Cook for 5 minutes, stirring occasionally, to blend flavours. Add fettuccine. Toss. Serves 4.

1 serving: 511 Calories; 21.7 g Total Fat (9.5 g Mono, 2.3 g Poly, 7.2 g Sat); 68 mg Cholesterol; 48 g Carbohydrate; 3 g Fibre; 31 g Protein; 920 mg Sodium

Pictured at right.

tip

It's easy to slice your meat more precisely if you first place it in the freezer until it is just starting to freeze (approximately 30 minutes). The meat will retain its shape and be quite easy to cut. If you are using meat that is already frozen, let it partially thaw before cutting.

Pineapple Beef Stir-Fry

Flank steak	1 lb.	454 g
Cooking oil	1 tbsp.	15 mL
Medium onion, cut into 1 inch (2.5 cm) wedges	1	1
Can of pineapple chunks (with juice)	14 oz.	398 mL
Brown sugar, packed	1/4 cup	60 mL
White vinegar	1/4 cup	60 mL
Chili sauce	2 tbsp.	30 mL
Soy sauce	1 tbsp.	15 mL
Water	2 tbsp.	30 mL
Cornstarch	2 tbsp.	30 mL
Medium tomatoes, cut into 8 wedges each	2	2
Medium red pepper, cut into 1 inch (2.5 cm) pieces	1	1

Cut steak with grain into 2 inch (5 cm) strips. Cut across grain into 1/8 inch (3 mm) thick slices.

Heat large frying pan or wok on medium-high until very hot. Add cooking oil. Add beef and onion. Stir-fry for about 3 minutes until beef reaches desired doneness.

Add next 5 ingredients. Stir. Bring to a boil. Reduce heat to medium-low. Simmer, covered, for 10 minutes.

Stir water into cornstarch in small cup. Add to beef mixture. Add tomato and red pepper. Heat and stir for about 2 minutes until boiling and thickened. Serves 4.

1 serving: 379 Calories; 10.8 g Total Fat (4.9 g Mono, 1.5 g Poly, 3.2 g Sat); 34 mg Cholesterol; 46 g Carbohydrate; 4 g Fibre; 27 g Protein; 644 mg Sodium

Pictured at right.

Clockwise from top:
Beef And Greens Stir-Fry, page 22
Indian-Spiced Beef, page 23
Pineapple Beef Stir-Fry, above

This is one dish that will have even the youngest members of the household eating their greens—and loving it! Great for a hurried weekday night.

pan-fried noodles

Simple to make and great topped with any stir-fry!

1. Cook 8 oz. (225 g) fresh, thin Chinese-style egg noodles in boiling salted water for about 2 minutes, stirring occasionally, until tender but firm. Drain.

2. Heat large frying pan on medium until very hot. Add 1 1/2 tbsp. (25 mL) cooking oil. Add noodles and 2 tsp. (10 mL) soy sauce. Mix well.

3. Flatten noodles into an even layer on bottom of frying pan. Cook for 3 to 5 minutes until bottom is golden brown.

4. Slide noodles out of frying pan onto plate. Cover with another plate. Invert and slide noodles back into same frying pan.

5. Sprinkle with 1/4 tsp. (1 mL) salt. Cook for another 3 to 4 minutes until noodles are crisp and golden.

Beef And Greens Stir-Fry

Cooking oil	2 tsp.	10 mL
Beef top sirloin steak, cut across grain into thin strips	1 lb.	454 g
Soy sauce	1 tbsp.	15 mL
Finely grated gingerroot (or 1/2 tsp., 2 mL, ground ginger)	2 tsp.	10 mL
Garlic clove, minced (or 1/4 tsp., 1 mL, powder)	1	1
Sliced fresh white mushrooms	3 cups	750 mL
Broccoli florets	3 cups	750 mL
Large onion, cut into 1 inch (2.5 cm) wedges	1	1
Water	1/2 cup	125 mL
Cornstarch	2 tsp.	10 mL
Beef (or chicken) bouillon powder	1 tsp.	5 mL
Green onions, cut diagonally into 1 inch (2.5 cm) pieces	4	4
Chinese five-spice powder, just a pinch		

Heat large frying pan or wok on medium-high until very hot. Add cooking oil. Add next 4 ingredients. Stir-fry for 2 minutes.

Add next 3 ingredients. Stir-fry for about 4 minutes until broccoli is tender-crisp.

Combine next 3 ingredients in small cup. Add to beef mixture. Heat and stir until boiling and thickened.

Add green onion and five-spice powder. Stir. Serves 4.

1 serving: 267 Calories; 10.7 g Total Fat (4.6 g Mono, 1.1 g Poly, 3.3 g Sat); 60 mg Cholesterol; 15 g Carbohydrate; 3 g Fibre; 28 g Protein; 409 mg Sodium

Pictured on page 21.

Indian-Spiced Beef

Ingredient	Imperial	Metric
Cooking oil	1 tbsp.	15 mL
Medium onion, coarsely chopped	1	1
Finely chopped gingerroot (or 3/4 tsp., 4 mL, ground ginger)	1 tbsp.	15 mL
Garlic cloves, minced (or 1/2 tsp., 2 mL, powder)	2	2
Ground cumin	1 tsp.	5 mL
Cooked lean beef, cut into 2 x 1/4 inch (5 x 0.6 cm) strips	2 cups	500 mL
Large ripe mango, diced	1	1
Medium tomato, chopped	1	1
Medium red pepper, cut into 1 inch (2.5 cm) pieces	1/2	1/2
Medium yellow pepper, cut into 1 inch (2.5 cm) pieces	1/2	1/2
Dried crushed chilies	1/2 tsp.	2 mL
Ground cardamom	1/4 tsp.	1 mL
Salt	1/4 tsp.	1 mL

Fit for a sultan, this spicy dish is given the royal treatment with chilies and the exotic tastes of cumin and cardamom.

Heat large frying pan or wok on medium-high until very hot. Add cooking oil. Add next 4 ingredients. Stir-fry for 2 minutes.

Add beef. Stir-fry for 1 minute.

Add remaining 7 ingredients. Stir-fry for about 2 minutes until heated through. Serves 4.

1 serving: 404 Calories; 15.7 g Total Fat (7.0 g Mono, 1.6 g Poly, 4.8 g Sat); 98 mg Cholesterol; 31 g Carbohydrate; 4 g Fibre; 36 g Protein; 202 mg Sodium

Pictured on page 23.

Don't walk away from that wok— this zesty stir-fry cooks up in about 10 minutes! To make this dish extra-special, serve it in home-made noodle baskets.

noodle baskets

A fun way to serve your stir-fries— and they're large enough to hold 5 cups (1.25 L) of stir-fry. Use 2 8 inch (20 cm) mesh wire baskets with long handles for deep frying the noodles (these can be purchased from an Asian grocery store or a kitchen supply store).

1. Separate 1 lb. (454 g) fresh thick yellow noodles (Mandarin noodles).
2. Place half of noodles in basket. Press another basket on top, forcing noodles into a bowl shape.
3. Heat cooking oil in wok or large, wide pot to 375°F (190°C).
4. Holding both handles together, submerge baskets in hot cooking oil.
5. Hold and cook for 2 to 3 minutes until crisp and golden.
6. Remove to paper towels to drain. Cool slightly. Carefully loosen noodles from basket with knife. Repeat with remaining noodles. Makes 2 baskets.

Pictured at right.

Orange Beef And Broccoli

Orange juice	3/4 cup	175 mL
Cornstarch	1 tbsp.	15 mL
Soy sauce	3 tbsp.	50 mL
Granulated sugar	1 tbsp.	15 mL
White vinegar	1 tsp.	5 mL
Beef top sirloin steak	1 lb.	454 g
Cooking oil	1 tbsp.	15 mL
Finely grated gingerroot (or 1/2 tsp., 2 mL, ground ginger)	2 tsp.	10 mL
Garlic clove, minced (or 1/4 tsp., 1 mL, powder)	1	1
Cooking oil	1 tbsp.	15 mL
Medium red onion, cut into thin wedges	1	1
Medium carrots, sliced paper-thin	2	2
Broccoli florets	2 cups	500 mL
Grated orange zest	1 tbsp.	15 mL
Medium orange, divided into segments, halved	1	1

Stir orange juice into cornstarch in small bowl. Add next 3 ingredients. Stir. Set aside.

Cut steak across grain into 1/8 inch (3 mm) thick slices. Cut slices into 2 inch (5 cm) strips.

Heat wok or large frying pan on medium-high until very hot. Add first amount of cooking oil. Add beef, ginger and garlic. Stir-fry for 3 to 4 minutes until beef reaches desired doneness. Transfer to separate small bowl. Cover to keep warm.

Add second amount of cooking oil to hot wok. Add onion and carrot. Stir-fry for 3 minutes.

Add broccoli and orange zest. Stir-fry until vegetables are tender-crisp.

Add beef mixture and orange. Stir cornstarch mixture. Add to beef mixture. Heat and stir until boiling and thickened. Serves 4.

1 serving: 435 Calories; 18.3 g Total Fat (8.6 g Mono, 2.6 g Poly, 4.8 g Sat); 83 mg Cholesterol; 31 g Carbohydrate; 5 g Fibre; 37 g Protein; 1109 mg Sodium

Pictured at right.

This dish ups the heat factor and flavour of a similarly-named takeout staple. Ordinary beef and broccoli will taste positively bland by comparison!

about kitchen shears

Want to get your kids involved in the cooking but don't think they're up to wielding knives like a Ginsu salesman just yet? Invest in a pair of kitchen scissors and let them help with cutting the more tender veggies. With a little practice and some supervision, they can cut green onions, celery, pea pods—you name it.

Spicy Beef And Broccoli

Egg white (large), fork-beaten	1	1
Cornstarch	1 tbsp.	15 mL
Dry sherry	1 tsp.	5 mL
Salt	1/2 tsp.	2 mL
Pepper	1/2 tsp.	2 mL
Hot pepper sauce	1/2 tsp.	2 mL
Beef inside round (or flank) steak, cut across grain into thin strips	1 lb.	454 g
Soy sauce	1 tbsp.	15 mL
Chili sauce	1 tbsp.	15 mL
Red wine vinegar	1 tsp.	5 mL
Granulated sugar	1 tsp.	5 mL
Cooking oil	1 tbsp.	15 mL
Sliced broccoli stems, cut diagonally into very thin slices	1 1/2 cups	375 mL
Garlic cloves, minced (or 1/2 tsp., 2 mL, powder)	2	2
Broccoli florets, cut lengthwise	1 1/2 cups	375 mL
Sliced fresh white mushrooms	1 cup	250 mL
Green onions, thinly sliced	4	4
Cooking oil	1 tbsp.	15 mL

Combine first 6 ingredients in medium bowl.

Add beef. Stir. Cover. Let stand for 10 to 15 minutes at room temperature, stirring occasionally.

Combine next 4 ingredients in small bowl. Set aside.

Heat large frying pan or wok on medium-high until very hot. Add cooking oil. Add broccoli stems and garlic. Stir-fry for 1 to 2 minutes until fragrant.

Add next 3 ingredients. Stir-fry for about 4 minutes until broccoli florets are tender-crisp. Transfer to separate medium bowl. Cover to keep warm.

Add second amount of cooking oil to hot frying pan. Add beef mixture. Stir-fry for 3 to 4 minutes until beef reaches desired doneness. Add soy sauce mixture and broccoli mixture. Stir-fry until bubbling and heated through. Serves 4.

1 serving: 274 Calories; 14.0 g Total Fat (6.8 g Mono, 2.3 g Poly, 3.4 g Sat); 34 mg Cholesterol; 9 g Carbohydrate; 2 g Fibre; 28 g Protein; 794 mg Sodium

Pictured at right.

This quick Japanese dish has become a perennial food-court favourite. But why fight the crowds at the mall when you can make it so easily, and so much better, at home?

food fun

Some of you may remember the Japanese love song called *Sukiyaki* that was popular in North America in the early sixties. Sung in Japanese by Kyu Sakamoto, this catchy tune was the first Japanese-language song to hit it big in America. But what about the name? Sukiyaki, all around the world, then and now, was and is considered to be a Japanese stir-fried beef dish—surely that's an odd title for a love song? It has been suggested that the American record producers renamed the song that was originally dubbed *Ue O Muite Aruko* (loosely translated as "I look up when I walk") to *Sukiyaki* simply because it was a Japanese word North Americans were familiar with!

Sukiyaki Rice Bowl

Prepared beef broth	1/2 cup	125 mL
Cornstarch	2 tbsp.	30 mL
Low-sodium soy sauce	1/2 cup	125 mL
Apple juice	1/2 cup	125 mL
Granulated sugar	2 tbsp.	30 mL
Cooking oil	2 tsp.	10 mL
Lean ground beef	1 lb.	454 g
Cooking oil	2 tsp.	10 mL
Large onion, cut into thin wedges	1	1
Sliced fresh white mushrooms	1 1/2 cups	375 mL
Shredded suey choy (Chinese cabbage)	2 cups	500 mL
Thinly sliced carrot	1 cup	250 mL
Can of bamboo shoots, drained	8 oz.	227 mL
Green onions, cut into 1 inch (2.5 cm) pieces	4	4
Hot cooked long grain white rice (about 1 1/3 cups, 325 mL, uncooked)	4 cups	1 L

Sliced green onion, for garnish

Stir broth into cornstarch in small bowl. Add next 3 ingredients. Stir. Set aside.

Heat large frying pan or wok on medium. Add first amount of cooking oil. Add beef. Stir-fry for about 10 minutes until no longer pink. Drain. Transfer to small bowl. Cover to keep warm.

Add second amount of cooking oil to hot frying pan. Add onion and mushrooms. Stir-fry for 5 to 10 minutes, until onion is softened.

Add next 4 ingredients. Stir-fry for 2 to 3 minutes until carrot is tender-crisp. Add beef. Stir cornstarch mixture. Add to beef mixture. Heat and stir for 1 to 2 minutes until boiling and thickened.

Spoon rice into 4 individual bowls. Spoon beef mixture over rice.

Garnish with green onion. Serves 4.

1 serving: 668 Calories; 21.2 g Total Fat (9.8 g Mono, 2.1 g Poly, 6.8 g Sat); 68 mg Cholesterol; 87 g Carbohydrate; 5 g Fibre; 32 g Protein; 1181 mg Sodium

Pictured at right.

Voila! *French cuisine—stir-fry style! All the fine flavours of the French classic in a fraction of the time. Serve over egg noodles. Bon appétit!*

Beef Bourguignon

Pearl onions	1/2 lb.	225 g
Water	3/4 cup	175 mL
All-purpose flour	2 tbsp.	30 mL
Dry (or alcohol-free) red wine	1/4 cup	60 mL
Beef bouillon powder	1 tsp.	5 mL
Salt	1/2 tsp.	2 mL
Pepper	1/4 tsp.	1 mL
Cooking oil	1 tbsp.	15 mL
Beef top sirloin steak, cut into 1/8 inch (3 mm) thick strips	1 lb.	454 g
Cooking oil	1 tsp.	5 mL
Small fresh white mushrooms (or 10 oz., 284 mL, can, drained)	2 cups	500 mL

Chopped fresh parsley, for garnish

Cook onions in boiling water in medium saucepan for 3 minutes. Drain. Plunge into ice water. Let stand until cool enough to handle. Gently squeeze each onion to push them out of their skins. Trim root ends. Set aside.

Stir water into flour in small bowl until smooth. Add next 4 ingredients. Stir. Set aside.

Heat wok or large frying pan on medium-high until very hot. Add first amount of cooking oil. Add beef. Stir-fry for about 3 minutes until beef reaches desired doneness. Transfer to small bowl. Cover to keep warm.

Add second amount of cooking oil to hot wok. Add onions and mushrooms. Reduce heat to medium. Stir-fry for about 5 minutes until onions are softened and mushrooms are browned. Add beef. Stir flour mixture. Add to beef mixture. Heat and stir for 2 to 3 minutes until boiling and thickened.

Garnish with parsley. Serves 4.

1 serving: 343 Calories; 20.9 g Total Fat (9.6 g Mono, 2.0 g Poly, 6.9 g Sat); 59 mg Cholesterol; 11 g Carbohydrate; 1 g Fibre; 24 g Protein; 308 mg Sodium

Pictured at right.

Is this a dish or a "wok" of art? With a rainbow of different peppers, this stir-fry might just be too pretty to eat—but too good to just look at. Serve over rice or noodles and let the dilemma be yours.

Three Pepper Stir-Fry

Ingredient	Imperial	Metric
Beef inside round (or sirloin) steak, trimmed of fat	1 lb.	454 g
Oyster sauce	2 tbsp.	30 mL
Garlic cloves, minced (or 1/2 tsp., 2 mL, powder)	2	2
Cooking oil	1 tbsp.	15 mL
Cooking oil	1 tsp.	5 mL
Sesame (or cooking) oil	1 tsp.	5 mL
Medium green pepper, cut into 1 x 2 inch (2.5 x 5 cm) pieces	1	1
Medium red pepper, cut into 1 x 2 inch (2.5 x 5 cm) pieces	1	1
Medium yellow pepper, cut into 1 x 2 inch (2.5 x 5 cm) pieces	1	1
Medium onion, cut into thin wedges	1	1
Celery ribs, thinly sliced	2	2
Prepared beef broth	1/2 cup	125 mL
Soy sauce	1 tbsp.	15 mL
Cornstarch	2 tsp.	10 mL
Brown sugar, packed	1 tsp.	5 mL
Dried crushed chilies	1/4 tsp.	1 mL

Cut steak lengthwise into 2 inch (5 cm) wide strips. Cut strips crosswise into 1/4 inch (6 mm) thick slices. Cut slices lengthwise into thin strips.

Combine oyster sauce and garlic in medium bowl. Add beef. Stir. Cover. Let stand in refrigerator for 1 hour, stirring occasionally.

Heat frying pan or wok on medium-high until very hot. Add first amount of cooking oil. Add beef mixture. Stir-fry for about 3 minutes until beef reaches desired doneness. Transfer beef to small bowl.

Add second amount of cooking oil and sesame oil to hot frying pan. Add next 5 ingredients. Stir-fry for 3 to 5 minutes until vegetables are tender-crisp. Add beef. Stir.

Combine remaining 5 ingredients in small cup. Add to beef mixture. Heat and stir until boiling and thickened. Serves 4.

1 serving: 278 Calories; 10.8 g Total Fat (5.1 g Mono, 2.2 g Poly, 2.3 g Sat); 48 mg Cholesterol; 18 g Carbohydrate; 3 g Fibre; 28 g Protein; 564 mg Sodium

Pictured at right.

Know some chaps you want to impress with this delightfully showy Korean noodle dish? Just pronounce it CHAHP-jee, and all the chaps will clap with glee!

about bean threads

Whether you call these noodles bean threads, Chinese-style vermicelli, *harusame*, cellophane noodles or glass noodles, one thing is certain—they have a very unique look! They are often called cellophane or glass noodles because of their translucent appearance. However, they are not noodles in the traditional sense because noodles typically contain flour, water and egg, whereas bean threads are made of mung bean starch. Bean threads generally require pre-soaking in hot water prior to being used in stir-fries and other dishes.

Chap Jae

Chinese-style vermicelli (bean thread), or rice vermicelli, broken up	4 oz.	113 g
Sesame (or cooking) oil	1 tsp.	5 mL
Lean ground beef	1/2 lb.	225 g
Green onion, sliced	1	1
Soy sauce	1 tbsp.	15 mL
Granulated sugar	1 tsp.	5 mL
Garlic clove, minced (or 1/4 tsp., 1 mL, powder)	1	1
Pepper, sprinkle		
Sesame (or cooking) oil	2 tsp.	10 mL
Thinly sliced carrot	1 cup	250 mL
Sliced brown (or white) mushrooms	2 cups	500 mL
Medium onion, thinly sliced	1	1
Chopped fresh spinach leaves, lightly packed	3 cups	750 mL
Cooking oil	1 1/2 tsp.	7 mL
Soy sauce	1 tbsp.	15 mL
Granulated sugar	2 tsp.	10 mL
Sesame seeds, toasted (see Tip, page 56), for garnish		

Put vermicelli into medium heatproof bowl. Cover with boiling water. Let stand for about 2 minutes until softened. Drain. Cover to keep warm.

Heat wok or large frying pan on medium-high until very hot. Add first amount of sesame oil. Add next 6 ingredients. Stir-fry for 3 to 4 minutes until beef is no longer pink. Transfer to large bowl. Cover to keep warm.

Add second amount of sesame oil to hot wok. Add carrot. Stir-fry for 1 minute. Add mushrooms and onion. Stir-fry for about 1 minute until carrot is tender-crisp. Add spinach. Stir-fry for about 1 minute until spinach is wilted. Add to beef mixture.

Add cooking oil to hot wok. Add vermicelli. Toss. Add beef mixture and second amounts of soy sauce and sugar. Stir-fry until heated through.

(continued on next page)

Garnish with sesame seeds. Serves 4

1 serving: 328 Calories; 13.1 g Total Fat (5.7 g Mono, 2.3 g Poly, 3.7 g Sat); 34 mg Cholesterol; 39 g Carbohydrate; 3 g Fibre; 15 g Protein; 754 mg Sodium

Pictured below.

Top: Chap Jae, page 34
Bottom: Szechuan Beef, page 36

Is it hot in here or is it just this stir-fry? Fans of flames will cheer for this tasty treat four-alarm style!

about szechuan cuisine

Think you know all there is to know about Chinese food from reading the menu at your local takeout? What many North Americans think of as Chinese cooking is actually made up of several distinctive culinary styles. One of the best known is the Szechuan style from the similarly-named province in Western China. Szechuan cooks like to heat up the kitchen with dishes like Kung Pao Chicken, Ma Po Tofu (tofu and ground pork in chili sauce), and Hot And Sour Soup, all of which are spiced up using ingredients like fresh and dried chilies and Szechuan peppercorns. So if you order a dish with Szechuan in its name, make sure you're ready to handle the heat!

Szechuan Beef

Beef inside round (or sirloin) steak	1 lb.	454 g
Soy sauce	3 tbsp.	50 mL
Dry sherry	3 tbsp.	50 mL
Finely grated gingerroot (or 1 1/2 tsp., 7 mL, ground ginger)	2 tbsp.	30 mL
Cooking oil	1 tbsp.	15 mL
Garlic cloves, minced (or 1/2 tsp., 2 mL, powder)	2	2
Chinese five-spice powder	1/2 tsp.	2 mL
Dried crushed chilies	1/4 tsp.	1 mL
Cooking oil	1 tsp.	5 mL
Julienned carrots (see Tip, page 110)	2 cups	500 mL
Julienned celery (see Tip, page 110)	1 cup	250 mL
Green onions, quartered lengthwise and cut into 2 inch (5 cm) pieces	8	8
Water	2 tsp.	10 mL
Cornstarch	2 tsp.	10 mL

Cut steak across grain into 1/4 inch (6 mm) thick slices. Cut each slice into 2 inch (5 cm) strips.

Combine next 7 ingredients in medium bowl. Add beef. Stir. Let stand at room temperature for up to 1 hour, stirring occasionally.

Heat large frying pan or wok on medium-high until very hot. Add second amount of cooking oil. Add next 3 ingredients. Stir-fry for about 4 minutes until vegetables are tender-crisp. Add beef mixture. Stir-fry for about 3 minutes until beef reaches desired doneness.

Stir water into cornstarch in small cup. Add to beef mixture. Heat and stir until boiling and thickened. Serves 4.

1 serving: 355 Calories; 21.9 g Total Fat (10.0 g Mono, 2.1 g Poly, 7.3 g Sat); 62 mg Cholesterol; 12 g Carbohydrate; 3 g Fibre; 26 g Protein; 1116 mg Sodium

Pictured on page 35.

Mandarin Beef

Low-sodium soy sauce	2 tbsp.	30 mL
Cornstarch	4 tsp.	20 mL
Oyster sauce	1 tbsp.	15 mL
Dry sherry	1 tbsp.	15 mL
White vinegar	1 tbsp.	15 mL
Granulated sugar	1 tbsp.	15 mL
Ketchup	1 1/2 tsp.	7 mL
Garlic powder	1/4 tsp.	1 mL
Cooking oil	1 tbsp.	15 mL
Beef top sirloin steak, cut into 1/8 inch (3 mm) thick strips	3/4 lb.	340 g
Green onions, halved lengthwise and cut into 2 inch (5 cm) pieces	4	4
Sesame seeds, toasted (see Tip, page 56), for garnish		

Stir soy sauce into cornstarch in small cup. Add next 6 ingredients. Stir. Set aside.

Heat wok or large frying pan on medium-high until very hot. Add cooking oil. Add beef. Stir-fry for about 3 minutes until beef reaches desired doneness.

Add green onion. Stir-fry until soft. Stir cornstarch mixture. Add to beef mixture. Heat and stir until boiling and thickened.

Garnish with sesame seeds. Serves 4.

1 serving: 235 Calories; 14.2 g Total Fat (6.6 g Mono, 1.4 g Poly, 4.6 g Sat); 40 mg Cholesterol; 7 g Carbohydrate; trace Fibre; 18 g Protein; 337 mg Sodium

Pictured below.

You're going to love the sauce! Serve over hot rice or noodles with a side of stir-fried vegetables to make a complete meal.

food fun

Ketchup has gone through many different phases over the past few centuries. This all-time favourite go-with is thought to have originated as a Chinese condiment called *ke-tsiap*—a spicy pickled fish mixture brought home by the British and renamed catsup. Over time, the ingredients were altered to include things like mushrooms and nuts. These mixtures were generally much thinner than the product we know. Some time in the late 1700s, tomatoes were added to the blend and ketchup, as we know and love it today, was renamed and reborn.

Supremely satisfying, with a touch of heat, this dish certainly lives up to its name! And we've made sure there's plenty of sauce to serve over rice or noodles.

about stir-fry vegetables

When making a stir-fry, think outside the bag. Be creative and design your own blend of favourite veggies rather than using a packaged stir-fry mix. Cut up broccoli, carrot, celery, cauliflower, zucchini, peppers or whatever suits your taste—as long as the volume used equals that listed in the recipe. Cutting your own vegetables will likely save money—however using pre-packaged blends of stir-fry vegetables has a time-saving benefit for busy lifestyles.

Chicken Supreme

Water	1 cup	250 mL
Low-sodium soy sauce	3 tbsp.	50 mL
Cornstarch	2 tbsp.	30 mL
Hoisin sauce	2 tbsp.	30 mL
Dried crushed chilies	1/2 tsp.	2 mL
Onion powder	1/2 tsp.	2 mL
Cooking oil	2 tsp.	10 mL
Boneless, skinless chicken breast halves, cut into bite-sized pieces	3/4 lb.	340 g
Cooking oil	1 tsp.	5 mL
Fresh mixed stir-fry vegetables	6 cups	1.5 L
Medium onion, cut into thin wedges	1	1
Garlic cloves, minced (or 1/2 tsp., 2 mL, powder)	2	2

Combine first 6 ingredients in small bowl. Set aside.

Heat large frying pan or wok on medium-high until very hot. Add first amount of cooking oil. Add chicken. Stir-fry for about 4 minutes until no longer pink. Remove to separate small bowl. Cover to keep warm.

Add second amount of cooking oil to hot frying pan. Add remaining 3 ingredients. Stir-fry for about 8 minutes until vegetables are tender-crisp. Add chicken. Stir cornstarch mixture. Add to chicken mixture. Heat and stir until boiling and thickened. Serves 4.

1 serving (250 mL): 221 Calories; 5.4 g Total Fat (2.4 g Mono, 1.7 g Poly, 0.8 g Sat); 50 mg Cholesterol; 21 g Carbohydrate; 5 g Fibre; 23 g Protein; 609 mg Sodium

Pictured at right.

Top: Chicken Supreme, above
Bottom: Chicken And Greens, page 40

Forget about the chicken and the egg, this is all about the chicken and the peanut! Smooth, spicy peanut sauce, chicken, tender-crisp veggies and chopped peanuts make this stir-fry extraordinary.

serving suggestion

Serve Chicken And Greens with Shanghai noodles cooked according to package directions, then fried in a little peanut or cooking oil until just brown and crisp.

Chicken And Greens

Low-sodium soy sauce	1 1/2 tbsp.	25 mL
Cornstarch	1 tbsp.	15 mL
Peanut sauce	2 tbsp.	30 mL
Oyster sauce	2 tbsp.	30 mL
Cooking oil	2 tbsp.	30 mL
Boneless, skinless chicken breast halves, cut into thin strips	1 lb.	454 g
Shredded suey choy (Chinese cabbage)	4 cups	1 L
Chopped bok choy	4 cups	1 L
Chopped unsalted peanuts	2 tbsp.	30 mL

Stir soy sauce into cornstarch in small bowl. Add peanut sauce and oyster sauce. Stir. Set aside.

Heat wok or large frying pan on medium-high until very hot. Add cooking oil. Add chicken. Stir-fry for 3 to 5 minutes until no longer pink.

Add suey choy and bok choy. Stir-fry for about 2 minutes until tender-crisp. Stir cornstarch mixture. Add to chicken mixture. Heat and stir for about 1 minute until boiling and thickened. Transfer to large serving dish.

Sprinkle with peanuts. Serves 4.

1 serving: 264 Calories; 12.7 g Total Fat (6.3 g Mono, 3.7 g Poly, 1.7 g Sat); 66 mg Cholesterol; 8 g Carbohydrate; 4 g Fibre; 30 g Protein; 369 mg Sodium

Pictured on page 39.

Sesame Chicken

Prepared chicken broth	1/3 cup	75 mL
Cornstarch	2 tsp.	10 mL
Soy sauce	1 tbsp.	15 mL
Sesame seeds, toasted (see Tip, page 56)	1 tbsp.	15 mL
Brown sugar, packed	2 tsp.	10 mL
Sesame oil (optional)	1/2 tsp.	2 mL
Peanut (or cooking) oil	2 tbsp.	30 mL
Boneless, skinless chicken thighs, cut into 3/4 inch (2 cm) pieces	1 lb.	454 g
Sliced leek (white part only)	2 cups	500 mL
Julienned carrot (see Tip, page 110)	1 cup	250 mL
Garlic cloves, minced (or 1/2 tsp., 2 mL, powder)	2	2

Stir broth into cornstarch in small cup. Add next 4 ingredients. Stir. Set aside.

Heat wok or large frying pan on medium-high until very hot. Add peanut oil. Add chicken. Stir-fry for about 4 minutes until no longer pink. Remove with slotted spoon to plate, leaving any excess oil in wok. Cover to keep warm.

Add remaining 3 ingredients to hot wok. Stir-fry for 2 to 3 minutes until tender-crisp. Add chicken. Stir cornstarch mixture. Add to chicken mixture. Heat and stir for 1 to 2 minutes until boiling and thickened. Serves 4.

1 serving: 301 Calories; 16.5 g Total Fat (6.7 g Mono, 4.8 g Poly, 3.5 g Sat); 76 mg Cholesterol; 15 g Carbohydrate; 2 g Fibre; 23 g Protein; 492 mg Sodium

Pictured on page 43.

When your family comes home to roost, serve them this impressive-looking dish. The subtle sesame sauce will really give them something to crow about!

about washing leeks

Talk about a high-maintenance vegetable! Getting leeks clean can be extremely exasperating. The only way you can get a leek truly clean is to cut it, rinse it and soak it. Remove and discard the green part of the leek and cut lengthwise through to the centre—without cutting it completely in half. Fan open the leek, letting its layers separate. Rinse between the layers. Place the leek in a bowl of cold water and let it soak for about ten minutes. Swish it around in the water to dislodge any last bits of dirt, then place it on a paper towel to dry. Whew!

You won't have to get up with the chickens to make this quick and easy stir-fry—it takes but minutes to prep and cook! The sweet, spicy glaze will have everyone asking for seconds!

about cornstarch

Cornstarch is, quite simply, the starch that comes from corn. Also known as cornflour, it is generally used as a thickening agent for sauces, gravies and puddings. It is, most often, mixed with a small amount of liquid before adding to a recipe—this helps to break up any lumps that may form. It's important not to heat cornstarch too high or stir too vigorously because it will start to thin under these circumstances. And never consider cornstarch a one-trick pony—cornstarch is actually very handy when it comes to cleaning up certain food mishaps. If you get a greasy stain on a non-washable item of clothing or on your carpet, dust the stain with cornstarch and let it absorb the grease. Brush it off when it has done its job.

Sweet Orange Chicken

Water	1 tbsp.	15 mL
Cornstarch	2 tsp.	10 mL
Cooking oil	1 tsp.	5 mL
Boneless, skinless chicken thighs, quartered	1 lb.	454 g
Thinly sliced carrot	3/4 cup	175 mL
Orange juice	3/4 cup	175 mL
Brown sugar, packed	1 tbsp.	15 mL
Balsamic vinegar	2 tsp.	10 mL
Hoisin sauce	2 tsp.	10 mL
Salt	1/8 tsp.	0.5 mL
Pepper	1/4 tsp.	1 mL

Stir water into cornstarch in small cup. Set aside.

Heat large frying pan or wok on medium-high until very hot. Add cooking oil. Add chicken. Stir-fry for about 5 minutes until browned. Add carrot.

Combine remaining 6 ingredients in small bowl. Add to chicken mixture. Stir. Bring to a boil. Reduce heat to medium-low. Simmer, covered, for about 6 minutes until chicken is no longer pink inside and carrot is tender-crisp. Stir cornstarch mixture. Add to chicken mixture. Heat and stir for about 1 minute until boiling and thickened. Serves 4.

1 serving: 229 Calories; 9.1 g Total Fat (3.6 g Mono, 2.3 g Poly, 2.2 g Sat); 76 mg Cholesterol; 14 g Carbohydrate; 1 g Fibre; 22 g Protein; 191 mg Sodium

Pictured at right.

Top: Sesame Chicken, page 41
Bottom: Sweet Orange Chicken, above

This classic is sure to be the "mein" attraction when family and friends chow down. Perfect served over steamed rice.

shrimp chow mein

Want a change from chicken? Omit the poultry and use 3/4 lb. (340 g) fresh uncooked medium shrimp, peeled and deveined. Stir-fry for about 1 minute until shrimp turn pink.

Chicken Chow Mein

Can of condensed chicken broth	10 oz.	284 mL
Cornstarch	2 tbsp.	30 mL
Low-sodium soy sauce	3 tbsp.	50 mL
Fancy (mild) molasses	2 tbsp.	30 mL
Cooking oil	1 tbsp.	15 mL
Boneless, skinless chicken breast halves, cut into thin strips	3/4 lb.	340 g
Cooking oil	1 tsp.	5 mL
Small green pepper, thinly sliced	1	1
Chopped onion	1 cup	250 mL
Chopped celery	1/2 cup	125 mL
Fresh bean sprouts	2 cups	500 mL
Can of sliced mushrooms, drained	10 oz.	284 mL
Can of sliced water chestnuts, drained	8 oz.	227 mL
Can of bamboo shoots, drained	8 oz.	227 mL
Dry chow mein noodles	1 cup	250 mL

Stir broth into cornstarch in small bowl. Add soy sauce and molasses. Stir. Set aside.

Heat wok or large frying pan on medium-high until very hot. Add first amount of cooking oil. Add chicken. Stir-fry for about 4 minutes until no longer pink. Transfer to separate small bowl. Cover to keep warm.

Add second amount of cooking oil to hot wok. Add next 3 ingredients. Stir-fry for 3 to 5 minutes until vegetables are tender-crisp.

Add next 4 ingredients and chicken. Stir-fry until heated through. Stir cornstarch mixture. Add to chicken mixture. Heat and stir until boiling and thickened.

Sprinkle with chow mein noodles. Serves 4.

1 serving: 360 Calories; 10.8 g Total Fat (4.3 g Mono, 4.1 g Poly, 1.6 g Sat); 50 mg Cholesterol; 40 g Carbohydrate; 7 g Fibre; 29 g Protein; 1233 mg Sodium

Pictured at right.

Time to shake it up and try something a little bit different. Balsamic vinegar adds a tangy sweetness to chicken and red onions. Serve over your favourite pasta.

about balsamic vinegar

You may have noticed that different brands of balsamic vinegar have different tastes. There's a good reason for this: in Italy, the process for making traditional balsamic vinegar is a closely-guarded secret. The ingredients are well known, usually just Trebbiano grapes with a little friendly bacterial culture to get the acidification started, but it's the process that is secret. Balsamic vinegar is aged for many years in a succession of kegs made from different aromatic types of wood. Each different wood flavours the vinegar in a unique way. What's kept confidential is what kinds of woods are used, in what order and how long the vinegar is stored in each one. You can imagine the almost limitless combinations!

Spicy Balsamic Chicken

Ingredient	Imperial	Metric
Cooking oil	1 tbsp.	15 mL
Boneless, skinless chicken breast halves, thinly sliced	1/2 lb.	225 g
Thinly sliced red pepper	1 cup	250 mL
Medium red onion, cut into thin wedges	1/2	1/2
Sweet (or regular) chili sauce	1 tbsp.	15 mL
Finely shredded fresh basil (or 3/4 tsp., 4 mL, dried)	1 tbsp.	15 mL
Garlic cloves, minced (or 1/2 tsp., 2 mL, powder)	2	2
Balsamic vinegar	2 tsp.	10 mL
Chili paste (sambal oelek)	1/2 – 1 tsp.	2 – 5 mL
Salt, sprinkle		
Pepper, sprinkle		

Heat wok or large frying pan on medium-high until very hot. Add cooking oil. Add chicken. Stir-fry for 3 minutes.

Add next 9 ingredients. Stir-fry for about 3 minutes until chicken is no longer pink and red pepper is tender-crisp.

Garnish with basil. Serves 2

1 serving: 247 Calories; 8.9 g Total Fat (4.5 g Mono, 2.6 g Poly, 1.0 g Sat); 65 mg Cholesterol; 14 g Carbohydrate; 2 g Fibre; 27 g Protein; 308 mg Sodium

Pictured at right.

Who says Sunday night dinner has to be cooked in the oven? Modernize your routine and put that baking time to better use (we know you want to!). This recipe gives you all the flavour of roasted chicken and stuffing without the long cooking time.

time-saving tip

Need to defrost frozen veggies quick? You can use the microwave but that sometimes results in veggies that are cooked before you want them to be. Another fast method, without the ill-effects of nuking, is to submerge the vegsicles in room-temperature water, changing the water when it gets too icy cool. Soon the veggies will be brought out of the ice age and will only require a good draining. This great trick also works exceedingly well with frozen shrimp.

Chicken 'N' Stuffing

Fine dry bread crumbs	1 1/4 cups	300 mL
Water	1/2 cup	125 mL
Parsley flakes	1 tsp.	5 mL
Poultry seasoning	3/4 tsp.	4 mL
Salt	1/4 tsp.	1 mL
Pepper, sprinkle		
Cooking oil	1 tbsp.	15 mL
Boneless, skinless chicken breast halves, cut into bite-sized pieces	3/4 lb.	340 g
Cooking oil	1 tsp.	5 mL
Julienned zucchini (see Tip, page 110)	1 cup	250 mL
Frozen peas and carrots	1 cup	250 mL
Chopped onion	1/3 cup	75 mL
Chopped celery	2 tbsp.	30 mL

Combine first 6 ingredients in small bowl. Reserve 1/4 cup (60 mL) crumb mixture. Set aside.

Heat wok or large frying pan on medium-high until very hot. Add first amount of cooking oil. Add chicken. Stir-fry for about 4 minutes until no longer pink. Transfer to separate small bowl. Cover to keep warm.

Add second amount of cooking oil to hot wok. Add remaining 4 ingredients. Stir-fry for about 2 minutes until vegetables are tender-crisp. Add chicken. Stir. Add larger amount of crumb mixture. Stir-fry until heated through. Sprinkle with reserved crumb mixture. Serves 4.

1 serving: 301 Calories; 8.0 g Total Fat (3.9 g Mono, 2.2 g Poly, 1.2 g Sat); 49 mg Cholesterol; 31 g Carbohydrate; 3 g Fibre; 25 g Protein; 495 mg Sodium

Pictured at right.

East meets southwest in this updated version of a family favourite. We've replaced the tortilla wraps with a sprinkle of corn chips for an extra crunch. Serve with extra salsa on the side.

Chicken Fajita Dinner

Lime juice	2 tbsp.	30 mL
Garlic cloves, minced (or 1/2 tsp., 2 mL, powder)	2	2
Dried crushed chilies	1/4 tsp.	1 mL
Salt	1/4 tsp.	1 mL
Pepper, sprinkle		
Boneless, skinless chicken breast halves, cut into thin strips	1 lb.	454 g
Cooking oil	2 tsp.	10 mL
Small red (or other mild) onions, sliced	2	2
Medium green or yellow pepper, sliced	1	1
Medium red pepper, sliced	1	1
Frozen kernel corn	1 cup	250 mL
Salsa	1 cup	250 mL
Water	2 tsp.	10 mL
Cornstarch	1 tsp.	5 mL
Corn chips (optional)	2 cups	500 mL

Combine first 5 ingredients in medium bowl.

Add chicken. Stir. Cover. Let stand in refrigerator for 1 to 2 hours, stirring occasionally.

Heat large frying pan or wok on medium-high until very hot. Add cooking oil. Add chicken mixture. Stir-fry for 3 minutes.

Add next 3 ingredients. Stir. Cook, covered, for 4 minutes, stirring occasionally.

Add corn and salsa. Heat and stir until mixture is hot and bubbling and chicken is no longer pink.

Stir water into cornstarch in small cup. Add to chicken mixture. Heat and stir until boiling and thickened.

Sprinkle with corn chips. Serves 4.

1 serving: 257 Calories; 4.7 g Total Fat (2.0 g Mono, 1.5 g Poly, 0.8 g Sat); 67 mg Cholesterol; 26 g Carbohydrate; 3 g Fibre; 29 g Protein; 418 mg Sodium

Pictured at right.

This unique version of the traditional black bean sauce is made with dried black beans instead of the usual soy beans. To save time, make the sauce a day in advance or use store-bought black bean sauce instead. Serve with brown or white rice.

tip

After garlic is cut and exposed to air, its chemicals start to break down and it begins to lose its pungency. To make sure your garlic keeps its kicky quality, cut immediately before using.

Chicken And Black Bean Stir-Fry

BLACK BEAN SAUCE

Dried black beans (see Note)	1/3 cup	75 mL
Boiling water	3 cups	750 mL
Water	3/4 cup	175 mL
Dry sherry	2 tbsp.	30 mL
Low-sodium soy sauce	1 tbsp.	15 mL
Garlic cloves, minced (or 1/2 tsp., 2 mL, powder)	2	2
Finely grated gingerroot (or 1/4 tsp., 1 mL, ground ginger)	1 tsp.	5 mL

STIR-FRY

Cooking oil	1 tsp.	5 mL
Boneless, skinless chicken breast halves, cut into long, thin strips	3/4 lb.	340 g
Cooking oil	1 tsp.	5 mL
Thinly sliced broccoli stems	2/3 cup	150 mL
Thinly sliced carrot	1/2 cup	125 mL
Small onion, cut into thin wedges	1	1
Sliced fresh white mushrooms	2/3 cup	150 mL
Broccoli florets, cut into bite-sized pieces	1 1/2 cups	375 mL
Snow peas, trimmed	1 cup	250 mL
Water	1 tbsp.	15 mL

Black Bean Sauce: Cook beans in boiling water in small uncovered saucepan for about 70 minutes until soft. Drain. Rinse beans. Drain. Remove 3 tbsp. (50 mL). Freeze remainder in 3 tbsp. (50 mL) portions for future sauce.

Bring beans and next 5 ingredients to a boil in small uncovered saucepan. Boil for about 15 minutes until reduced by half. Mash beans slightly with back of spoon while cooking. Makes about 1/3 cup (75 mL) sauce.

Stir-fry: Heat large frying pan or wok on medium-high until very hot. Add first amount of cooking oil. Add chicken. Stir-fry for about 4 minutes until no longer pink. Remove to small bowl. Cover to keep warm.

(continued on next page)

Add second amount of cooking oil to hot frying pan. Add broccoli stems and carrot. Stir-fry for 2 minutes. Add onion and mushrooms. Stir-fry for 2 minutes.

Add remaining 3 ingredients. Stir. Cook, covered, for 2 to 3 minutes until broccoli is tender-crisp. Add Black Bean Sauce and chicken. Stir. Serves 4.

1 serving: 185 Calories; 3.9 g Total Fat (1.7 g Mono, 1.1 g Poly, 0.6 g Sat); 50 mg Cholesterol; 12 g Carbohydrate; 3 g Fibre; 24 g Protein; 194 mg Sodium

Pictured below.

Note: To save time, substitute 3 tbsp. (50 mL) rinsed, drained canned black beans. Freeze remainder in small batches for future use.

Busy day? Toss together this quick and flavourful stir-fry and get back some precious "me time." Delicious over jasmine rice.

Easy Stir-Fry

Cooking oil	1 tbsp.	15 mL
Boneless chicken breast fillets (or boneless, skinless chicken breast halves), cut into short strips	3/4 lb.	340 g
Garlic clove, minced (or 1/4 tsp., 1 mL, powder)	1	1
Chili paste (sambal oelek), optional	1/2 tsp.	2 mL
Fresh mixed stir-fry vegetables	4 cups	1 L
Can of sliced water chestnuts, drained	8 oz.	227 mL
Thick teriyaki basting sauce	2/3 cup	150 mL
Dry sherry	1 tbsp.	15 mL
Soy sauce	1 tbsp.	15 mL

Heat wok or large frying pan on medium-high until very hot. Add cooking oil. Add next 3 ingredients. Stir-fry for 2 minutes.

Add vegetables and water chestnuts. Stir. Cook, covered, for 2 to 3 minutes until hot.

Add remaining 3 ingredients. Stir. Cook, covered, for 2 to 3 minutes, stirring occasionally, until vegetables are tender-crisp. Serves 4.

1 serving: 252 Calories; 5.1 g Total Fat (2.4 g Mono, 1.4 g Poly, 0.7 g Sat); 49 mg Cholesterol; 28 g Carbohydrate; 4 g Fibre; 23 g Protein; 1455 mg Sodium

Pictured on front cover and at right.

Life in need of a little zesty pick-me-up? Look no further than the citrusy flavour of tangy orange and the sweet subtlety of ginger in this pleasingly unforgettable stir-fry. Perfect served over rice.

tip

When toasting nuts, seeds or coconut, cooking times will vary for each type of nut—so never toast them together. For small amounts, place ingredient in an ungreased shallow frying pan. Heat on medium for 3 to 5 minutes, stirring often, until golden. For larger amounts, spread ingredient evenly in an ungreased shallow pan. Bake in a 350°F (175°C) oven for 5 to 10 minutes, stirring or shaking often, until golden.

Asian Citrus Chicken

Orange juice	3/4 cup	175 mL
Cornstarch	1 tbsp.	15 mL
Hoisin sauce	2 tbsp.	30 mL
Oyster sauce	1 tbsp.	15 mL
Rice vinegar (or lemon juice)	1 tbsp.	15 mL
Brown sugar, packed	2 tsp.	10 mL
Grated orange zest	1 tsp.	5 mL
Olive (or cooking) oil	2 tsp.	10 mL
Boneless, skinless chicken breast halves, cut into thin strips	3/4 lb.	340 g
Garlic cloves, minced (or 1/2 tsp., 2 mL, powder)	2	2
Ground ginger	1/2 tsp.	2 mL
Chopped onion	1 cup	250 mL
Chopped celery	1 cup	250 mL
Chopped carrot	2/3 cup	150 mL
Sugar snap peas, trimmed	2 cups	500 mL
Low-sodium prepared chicken broth	1/2 cup	125 mL
Sesame seeds, toasted (see Tip), optional	2 tsp.	10 mL

Stir orange juice into cornstarch in small bowl. Add next 5 ingredients. Stir. Set aside.

Heat wok or large frying pan on medium-high until very hot. Add olive oil. Add chicken. Sprinkle with garlic and ginger. Stir-fry for about 4 minutes until chicken is no longer pink.

Add next 3 ingredients. Stir-fry for 2 minutes.

Add peas and broth. Stir. Reduce heat to medium. Simmer, covered, for 3 to 5 minutes until carrot is tender-crisp and peas are bright green. Stir cornstarch mixture. Add to chicken mixture. Heat and stir until boiling and thickened.

Sprinkle with sesame seeds. Serves 4.

1 serving: 234 Calories; 4.2 g Total Fat (2.2 g Mono, 0.8 g Poly, 0.8 g Sat); 50 mg Cholesterol; 25 g Carbohydrate; 3 g Fibre; 22 g Protein; 257 mg Sodium

Pictured at right.

No one's going to leave the table hungry after you serve up this full-meal stir-fry. The simplicity of the sauce is perfect for more delicate palates.

tip

Celery looking a little bit wilted? Well, celery has amazing powers of rejuvenation—it can spring back to life even after you thought it was beyond all hope! Cut off the base or trim the celery ends if they are in separate stalks. Place each stalk upright in a container filled halfway with cold water. Walk away and let the magic happen. After an hour, your celery should be looking plump and robust. If it's still wilted and soggy, do not serve it. Just freeze it and use it the next time you are making soup stock.

Almond Chicken

Water	1/2 cup	125 mL
Cornstarch	1 tbsp.	15 mL
Low-sodium soy sauce	2 tbsp.	30 mL
Chicken bouillon powder	1 tsp.	5 mL
Cooking oil	1 tbsp.	15 mL
Boneless, skinless chicken breast halves, cut into bite-sized pieces	3/4 lb.	340 g
Sliced celery	1 cup	250 mL
Cooking oil	1 tsp.	5 mL
Fresh bean sprouts	2 cups	500 mL
Sliced fresh white mushrooms	1 cup	250 mL
Can of sliced water chestnuts, drained	8 oz.	227 mL
Hot cooked long grain white rice (about 1 1/3 cups, 325 mL, uncooked)	4 cups	1 L
Slivered almonds, toasted (see Tip, page 56)	1/2 cup	125 mL

Stir water into cornstarch in small bowl. Add soy sauce and bouillon powder. Stir. Set aside.

Heat wok or large frying pan on medium-high until very hot. Add first amount of cooking oil. Add chicken and celery. Stir-fry for about 4 minutes until chicken is no longer pink. Transfer to medium bowl. Cover to keep warm.

Add second amount of cooking oil to hot wok. Add next 3 ingredients. Stir-fry for about 2 minutes until mushrooms are soft and moisture is evaporated. Add chicken and celery. Stir cornstarch mixture. Add to chicken mixture. Heat and stir until boiling and thickened.

Spread rice on large serving platter or 4 individual serving plates. Spoon chicken mixture over top. Sprinkle with almonds. Serves 4.

1 serving: 490 Calories; 13.5 g Total Fat (7.5 g Mono, 3.5 g Poly, 1.4 g Sat); 49 mg Cholesterol; 63 g Carbohydrate; 5 g Fibre; 30 g Protein; 551 mg Sodium

Pictured at right.

With ground pepper, bell peppers and crushed chili peppers, this dish has been peppered every way imaginable!

about chopstick etiquette

Yes, just as with knives and forks, there are necessary manners when using chopsticks.

1. Double dipping is a no-no. Move food to your plate with the wider ends of the chopsticks. Just remember to turn them around before eating!

2. Don't pass food from one pair of chopsticks to another.

3. Don't spear food with chopsticks. If the food is larger than you can eat in one bite, pick up the piece with your chopsticks and bite off a portion.

4. If soup's on the menu, eat the solid ingredients with chopsticks, then use a traditional ceramic spoon to finish the broth.

5. Although they may increase your reach, don't use chopsticks to pull bowls or plates towards you.

6. Finally, remember that drum solos, walrus impersonations and impromptu fencing matches are always atrocious breaches of chopstick etiquette!

Peppered Chicken

Water	1 tbsp.	15 mL
Cornstarch	2 tsp.	10 mL
Soy sauce	2 tsp.	10 mL
Salt	3/4 tsp.	4 mL
Pepper	1/8 tsp.	0.5 mL
Boneless, skinless chicken breast halves, cut into 1/2 inch (12 mm) cubes	1 lb.	454 g
Cooking oil	1 tbsp.	15 mL
Medium green pepper, cut into 1/2 inch (12 mm) pieces	1	1
Medium red pepper, cut into 1/2 inch (12 mm) pieces	1	1
Dry sherry	2 tbsp.	30 mL
Soy sauce	1 tbsp.	15 mL
Dried crushed chilies (optional)	1/4 tsp.	1 mL

Combine first 5 ingredients in medium bowl.

Add chicken. Stir. Let stand at room temperature for 15 minutes, stirring occasionally.

Heat wok or large frying pan on medium-high until very hot. Add cooking oil. Add green pepper, red pepper and chicken mixture. Stir-fry for 7 minutes.

Add remaining 3 ingredients. Stir-fry for 2 to 3 minutes until chicken is no longer pink. Serves 4.

1 serving: 195 Calories; 5.5 g Total Fat (2.5 g Mono, 1.5 g Poly, 0.8 g Sat); 66 mg Cholesterol; 8 g Carbohydrate; 2 g Fibre; 27 g Protein; 1089 mg Sodium

Pictured at right.

Kung-Pow! This spicy Szechuan dish will hit your taste buds where it counts. Want a little less wow in your pow? Adjust the number of chilies to your preferred heat level.

tip

Hot peppers contain capsaicin in the seeds and ribs. Removing the seeds and ribs will reduce the heat. Wear rubber gloves when handling hot peppers and avoid touching your eyes. Wash your hands well afterwards.

Kung Pao Chicken

Water	2 tbsp.	30 mL
Cornstarch	1 tbsp.	15 mL
Hoisin sauce	1 tbsp.	15 mL
Soy sauce	1 tbsp.	15 mL
Chili paste (sambal oelek)	1/2 – 1 tsp.	2 – 5 mL
Soy sauce	1 tbsp.	15 mL
Cornstarch	1 tbsp.	15 mL
Boneless, skinless chicken breast halves (or thighs), diced	1 lb.	454 g
Sesame oil	1 tsp.	5 mL
Egg white (large), fork-beaten	1	1
Garlic clove, minced (or 1/4 tsp., 1 mL, powder)	1	1
Cooking oil	1 tbsp.	15 mL
Small carrots, thinly sliced	2	2
Garlic clove, minced (or 1/4 tsp., 1 mL, powder)	1	1
Finely grated gingerroot (or 1/8 tsp., 0.5 mL, ground ginger)	1/2 tsp.	2 mL
Diced green pepper	1/2 cup	125 mL
Diced red pepper	1/2 cup	125 mL
Green onions, cut into 1 inch (2.5 cm) pieces	3	3
Fresh small red chilies (see Tip), optional	1 – 5	1 – 5
Cooking oil	1 tbsp.	15 mL
Chopped salted peanuts, for garnish		

Combine first 5 ingredients in small cup. Set aside.

Stir second amount of soy sauce into second amount of cornstarch in medium bowl.

Add next 4 ingredients. Stir well. Set aside.

Heat wok or large frying pan on medium-high until very hot. Add first amount of cooking oil. Add next 3 ingredients. Stir-fry for 1 minute.

(continued on next page)

Add next 4 ingredients. Stir-fry for 1 to 2 minutes until peppers are tender-crisp. Transfer to separate medium bowl. Cover to keep warm.

Add second amount of cooking oil to hot wok. Add chicken mixture. Stir-fry for about 3 minutes until chicken is no longer pink. Stir hoisin sauce mixture. Add to chicken mixture. Heat and stir until boiling and thickened. Add pepper mixture. Heat and stir until peppers are coated and heated through.

Garnish with peanuts. Serves 4.

1 serving: 249 Calories; 10.1 g Total Fat (4.9 g Mono, 3.0 g Poly, 1.2 g Sat); 66 mg Cholesterol; 11 g Carbohydrate; 1 g Fibre; 28 g Protein; 811 mg Sodium

Pictured below.

Just call this fried rice galore. With veggies, chicken and ham, this great mix can be served as a side or dinner's star attraction. Can you think of a better way to use leftover rice?

Why do fried rice recipes call for cold cooked rice? When rice cools it becomes firmer and loses any excess moisture. Using hot cooked rice can result in a very mushy mess because hot rice will still absorb liquid. If your cold rice is clumping together, wet your hands slightly and break the clumps apart with your fingers—this will prevent the rice from sticking to your hands.

Chicken Vegetable Fried Rice

Cooking oil	1 tbsp.	15 mL
Boneless, skinless chicken breast halves, thinly sliced	3/4 lb.	340 g
Chopped green pepper	1 cup	250 mL
Chopped red pepper	1 cup	250 mL
Frozen peas	1 cup	250 mL
Can of sliced water chestnuts, drained	8 oz.	227 mL
Thinly sliced green onion	1/2 cup	125 mL
Chopped low-fat deli ham	1/2 cup	125 mL
Low-sodium soy sauce	1 1/2 tbsp.	25 mL
Hoisin sauce	1 tbsp.	15 mL
Sweet (or regular) chili sauce	1 tbsp.	15 mL
Cold cooked long grain white rice (about 2/3 cup, 150 mL, uncooked)	2 cups	500 mL

Heat wok or large frying pan on medium-high until very hot. Add cooking oil. Add chicken. Stir-fry for 3 to 5 minutes until no longer pink.

Add next 6 ingredients. Stir-fry for 2 to 3 minutes until peppers are tender-crisp.

Combine next 3 ingredients in small bowl. Add to chicken mixture. Stir.

Add rice. Stir-fry for about 5 minutes until heated through and liquid is almost evaporated. Serves 6.

1 serving: 228 Calories; 4.0 g Total Fat (1.8 g Mono, 1.1 g Poly, 0.6 g Sat); 38 mg Cholesterol; 29 g Carbohydrate; 3 g Fibre; 19 g Protein; 450 mg Sodium

Pictured at right.

Go green with this simple, but simply unforgettable stir-fry. The almonds and spice make it taste so right!

serving suggestion

Serve Broccoli Shrimp Stir-Fry over a lovely bed of rice and peas. Cook rice as directed but add frozen peas during the last 5 minutes of cooking.

Broccoli Shrimp Stir-Fry

Prepared chicken broth	3/4 cup	175 mL
Hoisin sauce	2 tbsp.	30 mL
Cornstarch	2 tsp.	10 mL
Chinese five-spice powder	1/8 tsp.	0.5 mL
Pepper	1/8 tsp.	0.5 mL
Cooking oil	1 tsp.	5 mL
Frozen uncooked medium shrimp (peeled and deveined), thawed	1 lb.	454 g
Cooking oil	2 tsp.	10 mL
Broccoli florets	3 cups	750 mL
Chopped green onion	1/2 cup	125 mL
Slivered almonds, toasted (see Tip, page 56)	1/4 cup	60 mL

Combine first 5 ingredients in small bowl. Set aside.

Heat wok or large frying pan on medium-high until very hot. Add first amount of cooking oil. Add shrimp. Stir-fry for about 1 minute until shrimp turn pink. Transfer to separate small bowl. Cover to keep warm.

Add second amount of cooking oil to hot wok. Add broccoli and green onion. Stir-fry for 1 minute. Stir cornstarch mixture. Add to vegetable mixture. Heat and stir for about 3 minutes until boiling and thickened and broccoli is tender-crisp.

Add shrimp and almonds. Stir-fry for about 1 minute until heated through. Serves 4.

1 serving: 252 Calories; 10.7 g Total Fat (5.4 g Mono, 3.1 g Poly, 1.1 g Sat); 173 mg Cholesterol; 11 g Carbohydrate; 3 g Fibre; 28 g Protein; 458 mg Sodium

Pictured at right.

An elegant stir-fry, indeed. Shrimp and artichokes in a decadent cream sauce—no one's going to believe you whipped this up in no time at all! When your guests ask how you did it, simply smile and say, "I just threw a few things in a frying pan." After all, you'll be telling the truth!

food fun

Artichokes are prized by many herbalists because they contain a chemical called cynarin that is thought to aid in liver functioning. And although cynarin has a sweet flavour, it is sometimes known to impart its sweetness in all the wrong places. Some people find that after eating an artichoke, everything else they eat soon after has an altered taste. Though this aftertaste may be quite pleasing if combined with the right foods, with the wrong combination it can be quite nasty (think of drinking orange juice right after you brushed your teeth!). So, consider saving that expensive bottle of wine to drink with a meal that doesn't contain artichokes.

Shrimp And Artichokes

Milk	1/2 cup	125 mL
Cornstarch	1 tbsp.	15 mL
Dry sherry	1 tbsp.	15 mL
Worcestershire sauce	1 tsp.	5 mL
Salt	1/4 tsp.	1 mL
Pepper, sprinkle		
Cooking oil	1 tbsp.	15 mL
Sliced fresh white mushrooms	1 cup	250 mL
Can of artichoke hearts, drained and halved	14 oz.	398 mL
Cooking oil	1 tsp.	5 mL
Frozen, uncooked medium shrimp (peeled and deveined), thawed	3/4 lb.	340 g
Grated Parmesan cheese	2 tbsp.	30 mL
Chopped fresh parsley, for garnish		

Stir milk into cornstarch in small bowl. Add next 4 ingredients. Stir. Set aside.

Heat wok or large frying pan on medium-high until very hot. Add first amount of cooking oil. Add mushrooms and artichoke hearts. Stir-fry for about 2 minutes until golden. Transfer to separate small bowl. Cover to keep warm.

Add second amount of cooking oil to hot wok. Add shrimp. Stir-fry for about 1 minute until shrimp turn pink. Add mushroom mixture. Stir cornstarch mixture. Add to shrimp mixture. Heat and stir until boiling and thickened.

Sprinkle with cheese and parsley. Serves 4.

1 serving: 223 Calories; 7.5 g Total Fat (3.3 g Mono, 2.0 g Poly, 1.4 g Sat); 133 mg Cholesterol; 16 g Carbohydrate; 5 g Fibre; 24 g Protein; 429 mg Sodium

Pictured at right.

The five-spice powder in this light and spicy dish gives a tantalizing touch of the exotic. Adjust the amount of chilies to suit your preference.

how to devein shrimp

If you happen to purchase shrimp that aren't already deveined, fret not—it's as easy to do as prepping vegetables. If your shrimp are still in the shell, start by stripping off the legs and peeling off the shell. Leave the tail intact, if desired. Using a small, sharp knife, make a shallow cut along the centre of the back. Rinse under cold water to wash out the dark vein. To devein shrimp that you want to cook in the shell, simply cut along the back right through the shell and remove the vein in the same way.

Serve this quick, easy-to-prepare dish with a bowl of jasmine rice. Double the ginger if you're a fan of the flavour.

Five-Spice Shrimp

Frozen, uncooked large shrimp (peeled and deveined), thawed	1 lb.	454 g
Garlic cloves, minced (or 1/2 tsp., 2 mL, powder)	2	2
Dried crushed chilies	1/2 tsp.	2 mL
Salt	1/2 tsp.	2 mL
Pepper	1/4 tsp.	1 mL
Chinese five-spice powder	1/4 tsp.	1 mL
Peanut (or cooking) oil	1 tbsp.	15 mL
Green onion, thinly sliced	1	1

Cut shrimp down back almost, but not quite, through to other side. Press open to flatten slightly.

Combine next 5 ingredients in large bowl. Add shrimp. Mix well.

Heat wok or large frying pan on medium-high until very hot. Add peanut oil. Add shrimp mixture. Stir-fry for 2 to 3 minutes until shrimp turn pink.

Sprinkle with green onion. Serves 4.

1 serving: 155 Calories; 5.4 g Total Fat (1.9 g Mono, 1.9 g Poly, 1.0 g Sat); 173 mg Cholesterol; 2 g Carbohydrate; trace Fibre; 23 g Protein; 461 mg Sodium

Shrimp And Asparagus Stir-Fry

Low-sodium prepared chicken broth	1/4 cup	60 mL
Cornstarch	1 tsp.	5 mL
Low-sodium soy sauce	1 1/2 tbsp.	25 mL
Chili paste (sambal oelek)	1/2 tsp.	2 mL
Cooking oil	2 tsp.	10 mL
Sliced green onion	1/3 cup	75 mL
Garlic cloves, minced (or 1/2 tsp., 2 mL, powder)	2	2
Finely grated gingerroot (or 1/4 tsp., 1 mL, ground ginger)	1 tsp.	5 mL

(continued on next page)

Frozen, uncooked medium shrimp (peeled and deveined), thawed	1 lb.	454 g
Fresh asparagus, trimmed of tough ends and cut into 1 inch (2.5 cm) pieces	1 lb.	454 g
Sesame seeds (optional)	1 tbsp.	15 mL

Stir broth into cornstarch in small bowl. Add soy sauce and chili paste. Stir. Set aside.

Heat wok or large frying pan on medium-high until very hot. Add cooking oil. Add next 3 ingredients. Stir-fry for 1 to 2 minutes until fragrant.

Add shrimp and asparagus. Stir cornstarch mixture. Add to shrimp mixture. Stir-fry for about 5 minutes until shrimp turn pink, asparagus is tender-crisp and sauce is boiling and thickened.

Sprinkle with sesame seeds. Serves 4.

1 serving: 179 Calories; 4.5 g Total Fat (1.7 g Mono, 1.6 g Poly, 0.6 g Sat); 172 mg Cholesterol; 9 g Carbohydrate; 2.2 g Fibre; 26 g Protein; 357 mg Sodium

Pictured below.

about trimming asparagus

To cut or to snap? That is the question. Everyone has their own method for trimming the tough, woody ends of asparagus. Some prefer to cut their spears at the point where the green colour begins to fade. Others prefer to snap the asparagus at the point where the woody end becomes pliable. No matter how you do it, consider saving the ends for making soup stock. Just place them in a resealable plastic bag and store them in your freezer until ready to use.

Aloha! Enjoy the island flavours of this tropical-tasting stir-fry. Coconut milk and macadamia nuts mingle well with delectable mahi mahi. Enjoy with a piña colada!

Island Fish Stir-Fry

Coconut milk (or reconstituted from powder)	1/2 cup	125 mL
All-purpose flour	1 1/2 tbsp.	25 mL
Dry (or alcohol-free) white wine	1 tbsp.	15 mL
Cooking oil	1 tbsp.	15 mL
Mahi mahi (or other firm white fish) fillets, cut into 3/4 inch (2 cm) cubes	3/4 lb.	340 g
Salt, sprinkle		
Pepper, sprinkle		
Chopped raw macadamia nuts (or almonds), toasted (see Tip, page 56)	1 tbsp.	15 mL

Slowly stir coconut milk into flour in small bowl until smooth. Add wine. Stir. Set aside.

Heat wok or large frying pan on medium-high until very hot. Add cooking oil. Add fish. Stir-fry until fish is opaque. Sprinkle with salt and pepper. Transfer to separate small bowl. Stir flour mixture. Add to hot wok. Heat and stir until boiling and thickened. Add fish. Stir gently until heated through.

Sprinkle with macadamia nuts. Serves 4.

1 serving: 190 Calories; 12.0 g Total Fat (3.6 g Mono, 1.3 g Poly, 6.3 g Sat); 62 mg Cholesterol; 3 g Carbohydrate; trace Fibre; 17 g Protein; 79 mg Sodium

Your dinner guests will be ecstatic when they see this colourful dish with a delightful mild curry flavour. (And when you find out how easy it is to make, you'll be pretty excited too!)

Shrimp Ecstasy

Water	1 tbsp.	15 mL
Cornstarch	2 tsp.	10 mL
Egg white (large), fork-beaten	1	1
Salt	3/4 tsp.	4 mL
Curry powder	1/2 tsp.	2 mL
Granulated sugar	1/2 tsp.	2 mL
Frozen, cooked medium shrimp (peeled and deveined), thawed	1 lb.	454 g
Cooking oil	1 tbsp.	15 mL
Medium onion, thinly sliced	1	1
Small red pepper, thinly sliced	1	1
Green onions, cut into 2 inch (5 cm) pieces and slivered lengthwise	4	4

(continued on next page)

Stir water into cornstarch in medium bowl. Add next 4 ingredients. Stir.

Add shrimp. Stir. Let stand at room temperature for 30 minutes.

Heat wok or large frying pan on medium-high until very hot. Add cooking oil. Add onion and red pepper. Stir-fry for 3 to 4 minutes until tender-crisp. Add shrimp mixture. Stir-fry for about 3 minutes until heated through.

Sprinkle with green onion. Serves 4.

1 serving: 181 Calories; 5.5 g Total Fat (2.3 g Mono, 1.8 g Poly, 0.6 g Sat); 173 mg Cholesterol; 7.5 g Carbohydrate; 1 g Fibre; 25 g Protein; 659 mg Sodium

Pictured below.

For those who like all that the high seas have to offer, this dish is sure to please three times over! This creamy catch is best served over pasta.

freezing seafood

Fish wrapped and stored in the freezer can generally be kept for 2 to 3 months. To thaw frozen shrimp or other seafood safely and quickly, place in a colander under tepid running water.
Do not refreeze. Treat thawed seafood the same as fresh seafood and don't keep it in the fridge for longer than a day. Once cooked, leftover seafood dishes should be eaten within 3 days.

Three Seafood Fry

Milk	1/2 cup	125 mL
Cornstarch	1 tbsp.	15 mL
Worcestershire sauce	1 tsp.	5 mL
Salt	1/4 tsp.	1 mL
Cooking oil	1 tsp.	5 mL
Medium onion, thinly sliced	1	1
Small green pepper, chopped	1	1
Sliced fresh white mushrooms	1 cup	250 mL
Cooking oil	1 tbsp.	15 mL
Frozen, uncooked medium shrimp (peeled and deveined), thawed	1/4 lb.	113 g
Tuna fillet, cut into 3/4 inch (2 cm) cubes	1/4 lb.	113 g
Imitation crabmeat (or crabmeat, cartilage removed)	1/4 lb.	113 g
Dry sherry	1 tbsp.	15 mL

Stir milk into cornstarch in small bowl. Add Worcestershire sauce and salt. Stir. Set aside.

Heat wok or large frying pan on medium-high until very hot. Add first amount of cooking oil. Add onion and green pepper. Stir-fry for 3 minutes.

Add mushrooms. Stir-fry for about 2 minutes until golden. Transfer to separate small bowl. Cover to keep warm.

Add second amount of cooking oil to hot wok. Add shrimp and tuna. Stir-fry until shrimp turn pink and tuna is opaque.

Add crab and vegetable mixture. Stir-fry until heated through. Stir cornstarch mixture. Add to seafood mixture. Heat and stir until boiling and thickened.

Stir in sherry. Serves 4.

1 serving: 176 Calories; 5.9 g Total Fat (2.9 g Mono, 1.8 g Poly, 0.8 g Sat); 71 mg Cholesterol; 12 g Carbohydrate; 1 g Fibre; 18 g Protein; 249 mg Sodium

Pictured at right.

Clockwise from top left:
Three Seafood Fry, above
Dilled Snapper Fry, page 76
Shrimp Creole, page 77

With snapper and vegetables in a creamy dill sauce, your guests will be snapping up this dish faster than you can snap your fingers!

how to grow herbs

The thing with buying fresh herbs, such as chives, is that you usually have to buy more than you need. You use a small amount in your recipe and the rest moulders away in your fridge. Stop throwing your money away on unused produce and invest it more wisely in a small indoor herb garden. Kits are widely available at your local greenhouse and come with a variety of herb combinations. It's the easiest way to decorate your house—and your plate—at the same time.

Dilled Snapper Fry

Low-fat plain yogurt	1/2 cup	125 mL
Lemon juice	1/2 tsp.	2 mL
Granulated sugar	1/2 tsp.	2 mL
Dried dillweed	1/2 tsp.	2 mL
Onion powder	1/4 tsp.	1 mL
Cooking oil	2 tsp.	10 mL
Frozen kernel corn	1 cup	250 mL
Fresh asparagus, trimmed of tough ends and cut into 1 inch (2.5 cm) pieces	1/2 lb.	225 g
Cooking oil	1 tsp.	5 mL
Small onion, sliced	1	1
Cooking oil	1 tbsp.	15 mL
Snapper fillet, any small bones removed, cut into 3/4 inch (2 cm) pieces	3/4 lb.	340 g
Chopped fresh chives (or 3/4 tsp., 4 mL, dried)	1 tbsp.	15 mL
Salt, sprinkle		
Pepper, sprinkle		
Snow peas, trimmed	2 cups	500 mL

Combine first 5 ingredients in small bowl. Set aside.

Heat wok or large frying pan on medium-high until very hot. Add first amount of cooking oil. Add corn and asparagus. Stir-fry for 4 to 5 minutes until tender-crisp. Transfer to medium bowl. Cover to keep warm.

Add second amount of cooking oil to hot wok. Add onion. Stir-fry for about 2 minutes until tender-crisp. Add to vegetable mixture.

Add third amount of cooking oil to hot wok. Add fish and chives. Stir-fry for about 4 minutes until fish is opaque. Sprinkle with salt and pepper.

Add vegetable mixture and snow peas. Stir-fry until heated through. Add yogurt mixture. Heat and stir until bubbling. Serves 4.

1 serving: 258 Calories; 9.0 g Total Fat (4.5 g Mono, 2.7 g Poly, 1.1 g Sat); 33 mg Cholesterol; 22 g Carbohydrate; 4 g Fibre; 24 g Protein; 83 mg Sodium

Pictured on page 75.

Shrimp Creole

Can of diced tomatoes, drained	14 oz.	398 mL
Ketchup	1 tbsp.	15 mL
Brown sugar, packed	2 tsp.	10 mL
Chili powder	1 tsp.	5 mL
Salt	1 tsp.	5 mL
Cayenne pepper	1/8 tsp.	0.5 mL
Cooking oil	2 tsp.	10 mL
Sliced green pepper	1/2 cup	125 mL
Sliced red pepper	1/2 cup	125 mL
Sliced yellow pepper	1/2 cup	125 mL
Sliced onion	1/2 cup	125 mL
Thinly sliced celery	1/3 cup	75 mL
Frozen, cooked medium shrimp (peeled and deveined), thawed	1 lb.	454 g

Combine first 6 ingredients in small bowl. Set aside.

Heat wok or large frying pan on medium-high until very hot. Add cooking oil. Add next 5 ingredients. Stir-fry for about 3 minutes until tender-crisp.

Add shrimp. Stir-fry for 1 minute. Add tomato mixture. Stir-fry until heated through. Serves 4.

1 serving: 193 Calories; 4.5 g Total Fat (1.7 g Mono, 1.5 g Poly, 0.6 g Sat); 173 mg Cholesterol; 14 g Carbohydrate; 3 g Fibre; 25 g Protein; 853 mg Sodium

Pictured on page 75.

Wherever you live, the spicy flavours of the Louisiana bayou are just a quick wok away. Best served over hot rice.

about bell peppers

Bell peppers are one of several varieties of sweet peppers. They come in a virtual kaleidoscope of colours including green, red, yellow, orange, purple and black. (An interesting side note is that all bell peppers start out green and mature into other colours.) When buying bell peppers make sure the skin is glossy and tight. Peppers will continue to ripen after being picked but sadly, like humans, older bell peppers will start to wrinkle. Remove from plastic before storing in your crisper.

How easy can a rice dish be? You'll never know until you fry! There's a reason this takeout staple never goes out of style—it's just too tasty!

chicken fried rice

For the chicken variation of this recipe, omit shrimp and add about 1 1/2 cups (375 mL) chopped cooked chicken.

Shrimp Fried Rice

Cooking oil	1 tbsp.	15 mL
Thinly sliced onion	1/2 cup	125 mL
Chopped fresh white mushrooms	1 cup	250 mL
Sliced green onion	1/3 cup	75 mL
Soy sauce	2 tbsp.	30 mL
Ground ginger	1/4 tsp.	1 mL
Salt	1/2 tsp.	2 mL
Pepper, just a pinch		
Cold cooked long grain white rice (about 1 2/3 cup, 400 mL, uncooked)	5 cups	1.25 L
Frozen, cooked baby shrimp, thawed	1/2 lb.	225 g
Large eggs	2	2
Water	1 1/2 tbsp.	25 mL

Heat large frying pan or wok on medium-high until very hot. Add cooking oil. Add onion. Stir-fry for about 2 minutes until onion starts to soften.

Add mushrooms and green onion. Stir-fry for about 2 minutes until mushrooms are softened and moisture is evaporated.

Add next 4 ingredients. Stir. Add rice. Stir-fry until heated through.

Add shrimp. Stir-fry until heated through.

Beat eggs and water in small bowl. Pour over rice. Stir-fry until eggs begin to set. Serves 6.

1 serving: 269 Calories; 5.0 g Total Fat (2.3 g Mono, 1.3 g Poly, 0.9 g Sat); 119 mg Cholesterol; 40 g Carbohydrate; 1 g Fibre; 14 g Protein; 714 mg Sodium

Pictured at right.

Top: Sweet-And-Sour Shrimp, page 80
Bottom: Shrimp Fried Rice, above

No one will sport a sourpuss when this family favourite is served. Spoon it over steamed rice. We swear you'll be sweet on it, too!

Sweet–And–Sour Shrimp

Water	2 tbsp.	30 mL
Cornstarch	1 tbsp.	15 mL
White vinegar	2 tbsp.	30 mL
Granulated sugar	2 tbsp.	30 mL
Low-sodium soy sauce	1 tbsp.	15 mL
Ketchup	1 tbsp.	15 mL
Salt	1/2 tsp.	2 mL
Paprika	1/8 tsp.	0.5 mL
Cooking oil	1 1/2 tsp.	7 mL
Large green pepper, diced	1	1
Cooking oil	1 1/2 tsp.	7 mL
Frozen, uncooked small shrimp (peeled and deveined), thawed	3/4 lb.	340 g

Stir water into cornstarch in small bowl. Add next 6 ingredients. Stir. Set aside.

Heat wok or large frying pan on medium-high until very hot. Add first amount of cooking oil. Add green pepper. Stir-fry for 1 minute. Transfer to separate small bowl. Cover to keep warm.

Add second amount of cooking oil to hot wok. Add shrimp. Stir-fry for about 1 minute until shrimp turn pink. Add green pepper. Stir cornstarch mixture. Add to shrimp mixture. Heat and stir until boiling and thickened. Serves 4.

1 serving: 165 Calories; 5.0 g Total Fat (2.2 g Mono, 1.6 g Poly, 0.6 g Sat); 129 mg Cholesterol; 12 g Carbohydrate; 1 g Fibre; 18 g Protein; 585 mg Sodium

Pictured on page 79.

Shrimp And Pea Stir-Fry

Cooking oil	2 tsp.	10 mL
Small onion, cut into thin wedges	1	1
Sugar snap peas, trimmed	2 cups	500 mL
Julienned carrot (see Tip, page 110)	1 cup	250 mL
Frozen, uncooked medium shrimp (peeled and deveined), thawed	1 lb.	454 g
Chopped fresh mint	3 tbsp.	50 mL
Sweet (or regular) chili sauce	3 tbsp.	50 mL
Lime juice	1 tbsp.	15 mL

This stir-fry certainly doesn't skimp on the shrimp! Please your palate with this light and unique combination of shrimp, peas, chili and mint.

Heat wok or large frying pan on medium-high until very hot. Add cooking oil. Add onion. Stir-fry for about 2 minutes until onion is tender-crisp.

Add peas and carrot. Stir-fry for 2 minutes.

Add remaining 4 ingredients. Stir-fry for 3 to 5 minutes until shrimp turn pink and carrot is tender-crisp. Serves 4.

1 serving: 192 Calories; 4.4 g Total Fat (1.6 g Mono, 1.5 g Poly, 0.6 g Sat); 173 mg Cholesterol; 11 g Carbohydrate; 3 g Fibre; 25 g Protein; 199 mg Sodium

Pictured below and on back cover.

Noodles, shrimp, veggies and the big bold taste of black bean sauce make this a one-dish meal your taste buds won't soon forget!

make it an asian feast

Give your dinner a touch of Asian inspiration in no time at all. Start dinner off with heat-and-serve spring rolls or egg rolls (available in your grocer's freezer), served with plum sauce for dipping. Follow with Black Bean Shrimp Noodles—eaten with chopsticks, of course. And for dessert, serve coconut ice cream with fortune cookies.

Black Bean Shrimp Noodles

Fresh, thin Chinese-style egg noodles	10 1/2 oz.	300 g
Black bean sauce (pourable)	1/2 cup	125 mL
Water	2 tbsp.	30 mL
Medium sherry	1 tbsp.	15 mL
Cornstarch	1 1/2 tsp.	7 mL
Granulated sugar	1 tsp.	5 mL
Cooking oil	2 tsp.	10 mL
Halved fresh white mushrooms	2 cups	500 mL
Fresh mixed stir-fry vegetables	4 cups	1 L
Finely grated gingerroot (or 1/2 tsp., 2 mL, ground ginger)	2 tsp.	10 mL
Frozen, uncooked medium shrimp (peeled and deveined), thawed	1 lb.	454 g

Put noodles into large heatproof bowl. Cover with boiling water. Let stand for about 5 minutes until softened. Drain. Cover to keep warm.

Combine next 5 ingredients in small cup. Set aside.

Heat wok or large frying pan on medium-high until very hot. Add cooking oil. Add mushrooms. Stir-fry for about 2 minutes until mushrooms start to brown.

Add vegetables and ginger. Stir-fry for 2 to 3 minutes until vegetables are almost tender-crisp.

Add shrimp. Stir-fry for 2 to 3 minutes until shrimp turn pink. Stir cornstarch mixture. Add to shrimp mixture. Add noodles. Heat and stir for about 2 minutes until boiling and thickened. Serves 4.

1 serving: 447 Calories; 6.8 g Total Fat (2.3 g Mono, 2.1 g Poly, 0.9 g Sat); 179 mg Cholesterol; 60 g Carbohydrate; 5 g Fibre; 36 g Protein; 616 mg Sodium

Pictured at right.

Top: Black Bean Shrimp Noodles, above
Bottom: Seafood In Black Bean Sauce, page 84

Even the sanest of sailors would walk the plank for this seafood lover's delight. Serve over rice or noodles.

about scallops

Scallops are molluscs with wavy, fan-shaped shells—which is where the term "scalloped edge" comes from. They range in colour from beige to creamy pink and should have a seawater smell to them. If scallops are white and odourless, they have most likely been soaked in a solution that plumps them up and increases their longevity. If your scallops appear sandy, give them a brief rinse but do not soak them or they'll absorb too much water. Scallops are also notoriously easy to overcook and should never be cooked for more than 4 or 5 minutes.

Seafood In Black Bean Sauce

Water	2 tbsp.	30 mL
Cornstarch	1 tbsp.	15 mL
Black bean sauce (pourable)	2/3 cup	150 mL
Dry sherry	2 tbsp.	30 mL
Cooking oil	1 tbsp.	15 mL
Medium onion, cut into thin wedges	1	1
Thinly sliced green pepper	1/2 cup	125 mL
Garlic clove, minced (or 1/4 tsp., 1 mL, powder)	1	1
Finely grated gingerroot (or 1/8 tsp., 0.5 mL, ground ginger)	1/2 tsp.	2 mL
Cooking oil	1 tbsp.	15 mL
Frozen, uncooked medium shrimp (peeled and deveined), thawed	3/4 lb.	340 g
Fresh (or frozen, thawed) small bay scallops	1/2 lb.	225 g
Finely shredded suey choy (Chinese cabbage)	1 cup	250 mL
Green onion, thinly sliced	1	1

Stir water into cornstarch in small bowl. Add black bean sauce and sherry. Stir. Set aside.

Heat wok or large frying pan on medium-high until very hot. Add first amount of cooking oil. Add next 4 ingredients. Stir-fry for 2 minutes. Transfer to separate small bowl. Cover to keep warm.

Add second amount of cooking oil to hot wok. Add shrimp and scallops. Stir-fry for about 1 minute until shrimp start to turn pink and scallops are turning opaque. Do not overcook. Add vegetable mixture. Stir cornstarch mixture. Add to seafood mixture. Heat and stir for about 2 minutes until boiling and thickened.

Arrange suey choy on serving plate. Spoon seafood mixture over top. Sprinkle with green onion. Serves 6.

1 serving: 183 Calories; 7.2 g Total Fat (3.4 g Mono, 2.3 g Poly, 0.8 g Sat); 99 mg Cholesterol; 9 g Carbohydrate; 1 g Fibre; 19 g Protein; 329 mg Sodium

Pictured on page 83.

Speedy Shrimp

Cooking oil	2 tsp.	10 mL
Frozen Oriental mixed vegetables, thawed	4 cups	1 L
Frozen, cooked small shrimp (peeled and deveined), thawed	1/2 lb.	225 g
Instant white rice	1 1/2 cups	375 mL
Boiling water	1 1/2 cups	375 mL
Chicken bouillon powder	1 tsp.	5 mL
Salt	3/4 tsp.	4 mL
Pepper	1/4 tsp.	1 mL

Heat wok or large frying pan on medium-high until very hot. Add cooking oil. Add vegetables. Stir-fry for 4 to 5 minutes until hot.

Add shrimp. Stir-fry for 1 minute.

Add remaining 5 ingredients. Stir. Reduce heat to medium-low. Cook, covered, for 1 minute. Remove from heat. Let stand for about 6 minutes until moisture is absorbed. Serves 4.

1 serving: 268 Calories; 3.4 g Total Fat (1.5 g Mono, 1.1 g Poly, 0.4 g Sat); 86 mg Cholesterol; 41 g Carbohydrate; 4 g Fibre; 16 g Protein; 832 mg Sodium

Pictured below.

In a rush and your tummy's rumbling? Consider this satisfying and speedy shrimp stir-fry your go-to when you need dinner on the table quick. In under 15 minutes, you and yours can go from hungry to superbly satisfied.

about instant rice

Know why instant rice cooks quicker than other types of rice? Instant rice is completely cooked and dehydrated prior to packaging. Although this speeds up the cooking process, the flavour and texture of the rice is different than its conventionally cooked counterpart and, generally, contains fewer nutrients. However, when you're pressed for time, instant rice fits the bill quite nicely.

This delectable dish combines favourites from the land and the sea in a decidedly delightful blend of shrimp, pork, vegetables and noodles.

food fun

Long, long ago when it was expected the man open his wallet on a dinner date, the fella's interest could often be gauged by what kind of meal he was willing to pay for. And a dinner that included a fine bottle of wine and some surf and turf was considered to be quite the success! The term "surf and turf" is defined as a main course consisting of meat with seafood. Although this could mean any combination of meat and seafood, the term is most typically used in reference to steak and lobster. In Australia, the term "reef and beef" means the same thing.

Shrimp And Pork Noodles

Fresh, thin Chinese-style egg noodles	7 oz.	200 g
Cooking oil	1 1/2 tsp.	7 mL
Soy sauce	2 tbsp.	30 mL
Cornstarch	2 tsp.	10 mL
Hoisin sauce	2 tbsp.	30 mL
Liquid honey	2 tbsp.	30 mL
Dry sherry	2 tbsp.	30 mL
Water	2 tbsp.	30 mL
Chili paste (sambal oelek)	1/2 – 1 tsp.	2 – 5 mL
Cooking oil	2 tsp.	10 mL
Frozen, uncooked medium shrimp (peeled and deveined), thawed	3/4 lb.	340 g
Cooking oil	1 tbsp.	15 mL
Medium onion, halved and cut into 12 wedges	1	1
Chopped red pepper	1 cup	250 mL
Garlic cloves, minced (or 1/2 tsp., 2 mL, powder)	2	2
Finely grated gingerroot (or 1/4 tsp., , 1 mL ground ginger)	1 tsp.	5 mL
Lean ground pork	3/4 lb.	340 g
Thinly sliced cabbage	2 cups	500 mL

Put noodles into large heatproof bowl. Cover with boiling water. Let stand for about 5 minutes until softened. Drain.

Add first amount of cooking oil. Toss. Cover to keep warm.

Stir soy sauce into cornstarch in small bowl. Add next 5 ingredients. Stir. Set aside.

Heat wok or large frying pan on medium-high until very hot. Add second amount of cooking oil. Add shrimp. Stir-fry for about 1 minute until shrimp turn pink. Transfer to separate small bowl. Cover to keep warm.

Add third amount of cooking oil to hot wok. Add next 4 ingredients. Stir-fry for about 1 minute until fragrant.

(continued on next page)

Add pork. Stir-fry for about 5 minutes until pork is no longer pink. Stir cornstarch mixture. Add to pork mixture. Stir-fry for about 1 minute until boiling and thickened.

Add noodles and cabbage. Stir-fry for about 2 minutes until cabbage is tender-crisp. Add shrimp. Stir. Serves 6.

1 serving: 411 Calories; 18.6 g Total Fat (8.4 g Mono, 3.0 g Poly, 5.0 g Sat); 130 mg Cholesterol; 34 g Carbohydrate; 2 g Fibre; 27 g Protein; 721 mg Sodium

Pictured below.

Mango tangos with pork, zucchini and snow peas in a creamy curry sauce. Serve it over angel hair pasta and your family will be dancing in their seats!

tip

Want to know the world's best kept secret for cooking perfect pasta? Are you sure? It's quite revolutionary. The secret is...make sure you are cooking your pasta in plenty of water. Yes, that's all. One of the biggest mistakes people make when cooking pasta is using pots that are too small and don't hold enough water—resulting in a sticky, mushy mess.

Curried Pork And Mango Sauce

Angel hair	10 oz.	285 g
Cooking oil	1 tsp.	5 mL
Pork tenderloin, trimmed of fat, cut into 1/2 inch (12 mm) thick medallions	1 lb.	454 g
Chili powder, sprinkle		
Cooking oil	1 tsp.	5 mL
Skim evaporated milk	1/2 cup	125 mL
Cornstarch	1 tbsp.	15 mL
Coconut extract	1/2 tsp.	2 mL
Cooking oil	1 tsp.	5 mL
Chopped onion	1 cup	250 mL
Curry paste (or 1/2 tsp., 2 mL, powder)	2 tsp.	10 mL
Diced zucchini	2 cups	500 mL
Can of sliced mango in syrup, drained and syrup reserved, diced	14 oz.	398 mL
Diced red pepper	1 cup	250 mL
Lime juice	1 tbsp.	15 mL
Paprika	1 tsp.	5 mL
Dried crushed chilies (optional)	1/4 tsp	1 mL
Reserved mango syrup	1/2 cup	125 mL
Snow peas, trimmed, sliced diagonally	2 1/2 cups	625 mL
Flaked coconut, toasted (see Tip, page 56)	2 tsp.	10 mL

Cook pasta in boiling salted water in large uncovered saucepan or Dutch oven for 5 to 6 minutes, stirring occasionally, until tender but firm. Drain. Return to same pot. Toss with first amount of cooking oil. Cover to keep warm.

Sprinkle both sides of each pork medallion with chili powder. Heat large frying pan or wok on medium-high until very hot. Add second amount of cooking oil. Add pork. Stir-fry until browned. Remove to plate. Cover to keep warm.

Combine next 3 ingredients in small cup. Set aside.

Add third amount of cooking oil to hot frying pan. Add onion and curry paste. Stir-fry for about 2 minutes until onion is softened.

(continued on next page)

Add next 6 ingredients. Stir. Cook, covered, for 4 minutes, stirring occasionally.

Reduce heat to medium. Stir cornstarch mixture. Add to zucchini mixture. Heat and stir until boiling and thickened. Add reserved mango syrup. Stir. Add pork. Simmer, uncovered, for 5 minutes.

Add snow peas. Cook for 2 to 3 minutes, stirring occasionally, until tender-crisp.

Serve over pasta. Sprinkle with coconut. Serves 4.

1 serving: 603 Calories; 8.6 g Total Fat (3.4 g Mono, 1.5 g Poly, 1.9 g Sat); 68 mg Cholesterol; 89 g Carbohydrate; 5 g Fibre; 41 g Protein; 106 mg Sodium

Pictured below.

Haven't mastered chopsticks yet? With this stir fry, the only utensils you'll need are your own two helping hands. Wrap this sweet and spicy pork filling in a tortilla for a quick lunch you can eat on the go.

exploring flour tortillas

Plain flour tortillas, while a trusty standby, are simply not as much fun as the flavoured varieties! Flavoured tortillas add an extra bit of oomph to your food while adding a splash of colour to your dinner plate. Most larger grocery stores should have a selection of the more common flavours. Generally, green tortillas are spinach flavoured, while red are tomato flavoured and orange are cheese flavoured. If you dare to explore even further, you may find other more exotic flavours like chipotle, pesto, jalapeño, habanero, cilantro and garlic. When choosing a tortilla, pick a flavour that will complement the entire meal, both in flavour and colour.

Peanut Pork Wraps

Cooking oil	1 tbsp.	15 mL
Thinly sliced red pepper	1 1/4 cups	300 mL
Sliced red onion	2/3 cup	150 mL
Garlic clove, minced (or 1/4 tsp., 1 mL, powder)	1	1
Finely grated gingerroot	1/4 tsp.	1 mL
Chopped cooked pork (about 9 oz., 255 g)	1 1/2 cups	375 mL
Pineapple tidbits, drained	2/3 cup	150 mL
Salted peanuts, coarsely chopped	1/3 cup	75 mL
Water	1/3 cup	75 mL
Oyster sauce	2 tbsp.	30 mL
Sweet chili sauce	2 tbsp.	30 mL
Sour cream	1/3 cup	75 mL
Sweet chili sauce	2 tbsp.	30 mL
Tomato (or spinach) flour tortillas (9 inch, 22 cm, diameter)	4	4
Fresh bean sprouts	1 1/3 cups	325 mL

Heat large frying pan or wok on medium-high until very hot. Add cooking oil. Add next 4 ingredients. Stir-fry for 2 to 3 minutes until vegetables are tender-crisp.

Add next 6 ingredients. Stir-fry for about 3 minutes until liquid is almost evaporated. Set aside.

Combine sour cream and second amount of chili sauce in small bowl.

Spread sour cream mixture down centre of tortillas.

Layer pork mixture and bean sprouts down centre of tortillas to 2 inches (5 cm) from bottom. Fold bottom ends of tortillas over filling. Fold in sides, leaving top ends open. Makes 4 wraps.

1 wrap: 480 Calories; 20.5 g Total Fat (6.2 g Mono, 1.9 g Poly, 6.6 g Sat); 68 mg Cholesterol; 47 g Carbohydrate; 3 g Fibre; 25 g Protein; 994 mg Sodium

Pictured at right.

Top: Sesame Pork Stir-Fry, page 92
Bottom: Peanut Pork Wraps, above

Just speak those magical words, "open sesame," and you'll discover a treasure trove of pork and onions in a golden ginger sauce. Simply sensational.

make it a meal

Serve over chow mein noodles, cooked according to package directions, tossed with a small amount of sesame oil and chopped green onion. Add a side of steamed sugar snap peas and sliced carrots.

Sesame Pork Stir-Fry

Prepared chicken broth	1/3 cup	75 mL
Hoisin sauce	3 tbsp.	50 mL
Low-sodium soy sauce	1 1/2 tbsp.	25 mL
Cornstarch	2 tsp.	10 mL
Cooking oil	1 tbsp.	15 mL
Pork tenderloin, trimmed of fat, cut into thin strips	1 lb.	454 g
Cooking oil	1 tbsp.	15 mL
Medium onions, cut into thin wedges	2	2
Finely grated gingerroot (or 1/2 tsp., 2 mL, ground ginger)	2 tsp.	10 mL
Sesame seeds, toasted (see Tip, page 56)	2 tsp.	10 mL

Combine first 4 ingredients in small bowl. Set aside.

Heat wok or large frying pan on medium-high until very hot. Add first amount of cooking oil. Add pork. Stir-fry for about 5 minutes until starting to brown. Transfer to separate small bowl. Cover to keep warm.

Add second amount of cooking oil to hot wok. Add onion and ginger. Stir-fry for about 3 minutes until onion is tender-crisp. Stir cornstarch mixture. Add to onion mixture. Add pork. Heat and stir for about 1 minute until sauce is boiling and thickened.

Sprinkle with sesame seeds. Serves 4.

1 serving: 289 Calories; 11.0 g Total Fat (5.8 g Mono, 2.9 g Poly, 1.7 g Sat); 67 mg Cholesterol; 17 g Carbohydrate; 2 g Fibre; 29 g Protein; 494 mg Sodium

Pictured on page 91.

Chili, Pork And Pear Stir-Fry

Hoisin sauce	2 tbsp.	30 mL
Dry sherry	2 tbsp.	30 mL
Soy sauce	1 tbsp.	15 mL
Cornstarch	1 tbsp.	15 mL
Cooking oil	1 tsp.	5 mL
Pork tenderloin, trimmed of fat, thinly sliced	1 lb.	454 g
Prepared chicken broth (or water)	2 tbsp.	30 mL
Garlic cloves, minced (or 1/2 tsp., 2 mL, powder)	2	2
Fresh small red chilies, finely chopped (see Tip, page 62)	2	2
Chinese five-spice powder	1/8 tsp.	0.5 mL
Sugar snap peas, trimmed	2 cups	500 mL
Can of pear halves in juice, drained and sliced	14 oz.	398 mL
Green onions, cut into 1 inch (2.5 cm) pieces	8	8
Sesame seeds, toasted (see Tip, page 56), optional	2 tsp.	10 mL

Combine first 4 ingredients in small bowl. Set aside.

Heat wok or large frying pan on medium-high until very hot. Add cooking oil. Add pork. Stir-fry for 3 to 5 minutes until browned. Transfer to separate small bowl. Cover to keep warm.

Add broth to hot wok. Add next 3 ingredients. Heat and stir for about 1 minute until fragrant.

Add pork and next 3 ingredients. Stir-fry for about 3 minutes until peas are tender-crisp. Stir cornstarch mixture. Add to pork mixture. Heat and stir until boiling and thickened.

Sprinkle with sesame seeds. Serves 4.

1 serving: 277 Calories; 4.5 g Total Fat (2.1 g Mono, 0.9 g Poly, 1.1 g Sat); 67 mg Cholesterol; 27 g Carbohydrate; 5 g Fibre; 30 g Protein; 547 mg Sodium

Pictured on page 95.

Pears and pork make tasty partners in this light stir-fry with a hot pepper zing and a hint of exotic Chinese five-spice.

about sesame seeds

Good things do, indeed, come in small packages. Tiny sesame seeds are rich in the powerful anti-oxidant lignan, which is best utilized by the body when the seeds are ground. Grown for thousands of years in Asia, these healthy and delicious seeds have brown, red, black and ivory varieties. The nutty and slightly sweet flavour of the seed lends itself to both sweet and savoury dishes. Due to their high fat content, they can turn rancid quickly and should be purchased in small quantities and stored in airtight containers in a dark cupboard for up to 3 months, in the refrigerator for up to 6 months or in a freezer for well over a year!

You'll be especially pleased at how quickly you can whip up this quick and easy treat. We don't call it special for nothing!

about wok chuans

Wok what? You may be asking. Wok chuans are specialized wok spatulas or wok shovels designed specifically to work with a wok's uniquely-rounded shape. Like a regular spatula it has a long handle but its base is quite different: the tip is rounded so it can easily fit against the wok sides; and instead of being flat, the edges curve up slightly to hold food better. Is it necessary to have a wok chuan if you are stir-frying? Not at all, it's simply more convenient. But beware, if you have a wok with non-stick coating, it is better to use a wooden spoon that won't destroy the finish.

Special Ham Fried Rice

Cooking oil	1 tbsp.	15 mL
Chopped onion	2/3 cup	150 mL
Chopped celery	2/3 cup	150 mL
Cooking oil	1 tbsp.	15 mL
Large eggs	2	2
Pepper	1/8 tsp.	0.5 mL
Cold cooked long grain white rice (about 1 cup, 250 mL, uncooked)	3 cups	750 mL
Chopped cooked ham (about 6 oz., 170 g)	1 cup	250 mL
Soy sauce	2 tbsp.	30 mL
Frozen peas, thawed	1/2 cup	125 mL
Green onions, sliced	2	2

Heat wok or large frying pan on medium-high until very hot. Add first amount of cooking oil. Add onion and celery. Stir-fry for about 3 minutes until tender-crisp. Transfer to small bowl. Cover to keep warm.

Add second amount of cooking oil to hot wok. Add eggs and pepper. Break yolks but do not scramble. Cook, without stirring, for 1 minute. Turn. Chop egg with edge of pancake lifter until egg is in small pieces and starting to brown.

Add next 3 ingredients. Stir-fry for about 2 minutes, breaking up rice, until dry and starting to brown.

Add onion mixture, peas and green onion. Stir-fry for about 1 minute until heated through. Serves 4.

1 serving: 334 Calories; 11.9 g Total Fat (6.2 g Mono, 2.8 g Poly, 2.1 g Sat); 115 mg Cholesterol; 41 g Carbohydrate; 2 g Fibre; 15 g Protein; 1170 mg Sodium

Pictured at right.

Top: Chili, Pork And Pear Stir-Fry, page 93
Bottom: Special Ham Fried Rice, above

Feeling saucy? Why not put a little pork on your fork? (Or chopsticks, as the case may be!) This dish is so full of sweet, saucy flavour, your family and friends are sure to ask for more.

Rice noodles are a popular type of Asian noodle that are traditionally served stir-fried or in soups. They tend to be a bit chewy and white in colour. Cooking rice noodles on the stovetop in boiling water is not the recommended method—this often causes the noodles to clump together. Instead, soak rice noodles in hot water until they soften. The thicker the noodle, the longer it will take to soften. Once they are softened, they're ready for stir-frying—just remember to drain them well.

Saucy Asian Dinner

Rice vermicelli, broken up	6 oz.	170 g
Water	1 cup	250 mL
Soy sauce	3 tbsp.	50 mL
Liquid honey	2 tbsp.	30 mL
Cornstarch	4 tsp.	20 mL
Hoisin sauce	1 tbsp.	15 mL
Garlic cloves, minced (or 1/2 tsp., 2 mL, powder)	2	2
Chili paste (sambal oelek)	1/2 tsp.	2 mL
Cooking oil	1 tbsp.	15 mL
Pork tenderloin, trimmed of fat, cut into 1/2 inch (12 mm) cubes	1 lb.	454 g
Fresh mixed stir-fry vegetables	4 cups	1 L
Sliced green onion (optional)	1/4 cup	60 mL

Put vermicelli into medium heatproof bowl. Cover with boiling water. Let stand for about 2 minutes until softened. Drain. Cover to keep warm.

Combine next 7 ingredients in small bowl. Set aside.

Heat wok or large frying pan on medium-high until very hot. Add cooking oil. Add pork. Stir-fry for 3 minutes.

Add vegetables. Stir-fry for 3 to 4 minutes until vegetables are tender-crisp. Stir cornstarch mixture. Add to pork mixture. Heat and stir for about 4 minutes until boiling and thickened. Add vermicelli. Toss. Cook for 2 to 3 minutes until heated through.

Sprinkle with green onion. Serves 4.

1 serving: 423 Calories; 6.7 g Total Fat (3.3 g Mono, 1.5 g Poly, 1.3 g Sat); 67 mg Cholesterol; 53 g Carbohydrate; 3 g Fibre; 33 g Protein; 1153 mg Sodium

Pictured at right.

This dish is sold by Thai street vendors any time, day or night. So in true Thai tradition, we suggest you whip this up for breakfast, lunch, dinner or a midnight snack!

food fun

Pad Thai is perhaps one of the most popular and well-known Thai dishes. In Thailand, it is sold by vendors in the streets as a quick and light meal. Pad Thai can have a number of different garnishes, typically nuts, cilantro and a wedge of lime. But you may also see cucumber, bean sprouts, green onion and lemon wedges as well. If you want to make your Pad Thai truly Thai-rrific, consider placing the whole gamut of garnishes on your table and letting your nearest and dearest dress their dinners as they please.

Pad Thai

Medium rice stick noodles	8 oz.	225 g
Cooking oil	2 tbsp.	30 mL
Garlic cloves, minced (or 3/4 tsp., 4 mL, powder)	3	3
Lean ground pork	1/4 lb.	113 g
Chopped uncooked shrimp (peeled and deveined)	1/2 cup	125 mL
Fish sauce	1 tbsp.	15 mL
Brown sugar, packed	2 tsp.	10 mL
Chili paste (sambal oelek)	1 tsp.	5 mL
Large eggs	2	2
Fish sauce	1 tbsp.	15 mL
Medium lime, cut in half	1	1
Fresh bean sprouts	1 1/2 cups	375 mL
Green onions, sliced	4	4
Unsalted peanuts, coarsely chopped	1/4 cup	60 mL

Chopped fresh bean sprouts, for garnish
Chopped unsalted peanuts, for garnish
Chopped fresh cilantro, for garnish
Diced English cucumber, for garnish
Lemon wedges, for garnish
Lime wedges, for garnish

Put noodles into large heatproof bowl. Cover with boiling water. Let stand for about 30 minutes until softened. Drain. Cover to keep warm.

Heat wok or large frying pan on medium-high until very hot. Add cooking oil. Add garlic. Stir-fry until golden.

Add pork. Stir-fry for about 1 minute until browned.

Add shrimp. Stir-fry for about 1 minute until shrimp turn pink.

Add next 3 ingredients. Stir. Make a well in center.

(continued on next page.)

Add eggs to well. Break yolks. Cook, without stirring, until partially set. Stir-fry until set.

Add noodles. Stir-fry until heated through. Add second amount of fish sauce. Stir. Squeeze juice from lime halves over mixture.

Add next 3 ingredients. Stir-fry until heated through. Arrange on platter.

Garnish with remaining 6 ingredients Serves 4.

1 serving: 491 Calories; 20.9 g Total Fat (10.2 g Mono, 4.7 g Poly, 4.4 g Sat); 156 mg Cholesterol; 56 g Carbohydrate; 3 g Fibre; 20 g Protein; 882 mg Sodium

Pictured below.

Sensational pork and pineapple tidbits soaking in a scrumptious sweet and sour sauce. Simply superb! Best served over steamed rice.

exploring rice

Feeling like your rice selection is a little limited? There are actually many types of rice available for you to sample. However, be aware that different types of rice have different cooking times, so plan your meal accordingly. Some kinds you may want to try include:

- Basmati
- Black
- Brown
- Carolina
- Della
- Jasmine
- Kalijira
- Wehani
- Wild Pecan

Sweet–And–Sour Pork

White vinegar	3 tbsp.	50 mL
Cornstarch	4 tsp.	20 mL
Cooking oil	1 tbsp.	15 mL
Pork tenderloin, trimmed of fat, cut into 3/4 inch (2 cm) cubes	1 1/4 lbs.	560 g
Medium carrots, thinly sliced	2	2
Medium green pepper, cut into strips	1	1
Medium onion, coarsely chopped	1	1
Water	1/4 cup	60 mL
Salt	1/2 tsp.	2 mL
Can of pineapple tidbits (with juice)	14 oz.	398 mL
Brown sugar, packed	1/3 cup	75 mL
Soy sauce	1 1/2 tbsp.	25 mL

Stir vinegar into cornstarch in small cup. Set aside.

Heat wok or large frying pan on medium-high until very hot. Add cooking oil. Add pork. Stir-fry for about 5 minutes until lightly browned.

Add next 5 ingredients. Cook, covered, for about 3 minutes, stirring occasionally, until vegetables are tender-crisp.

Add remaining 3 ingredients. Stir. Stir cornstarch mixture. Add to pork mixture. Heat and stir for 3 to 4 minutes until boiling and thickened. Serves 6.

1 serving: 250 Calories; 4.8 g Total Fat (2.4 g Mono, 1.0 g Poly, 1.0 g Sat); 55 mg Cholesterol; 28 g Carbohydrate; 2 g Fibre; 23 g Protein; 554 mg Sodium

Pictured at right.

You won't Thai up the stove for long when you make this light and fresh-tasting noodle bowl. Adjust the amounts of chili and soy sauce to suit your taste.

Lemon Grass Pork Bowl

Rice vermicelli	9 oz.	255 g
Soy sauce	1 tbsp.	15 mL
Cornstarch	2 tsp.	10 mL
Fish sauce	3 tbsp.	50 mL
Sweet chili sauce	2 tbsp.	30 mL
Water	2 tbsp.	30 mL
Cooking oil	2 tbsp.	30 mL
Boneless pork shoulder butt steak, cut across grain into 1/8 inch (3 mm) thick slices	3/4 lb.	340 g
Stalk of lemon grass, bulb only (root and stalk removed), bruised and finely chopped (or 1 tsp., 5 mL, grated lemon zest)	1	1
Garlic cloves, minced (or 1/2 tsp., 2 mL, powder)	2	2
Dried crushed chilies	1/4 tsp.	1 mL
Medium onion, cut into thin wedges	1	1
Medium carrot, julienned (see Tip, page 110)	1	1
Sliced English cucumber, halved	1/3 cup	75 mL
Fresh mint leaves	8	8
Fresh bean sprouts	1/2 cup	125 mL
Shredded iceberg lettuce, lightly packed	1/2 cup	125 mL
Thinly sliced green onion	1/4 cup	60 mL
Chopped dry-roasted peanuts	1/4 cup	60 mL

Put vermicelli into large heatproof bowl. Cover with boiling water. Let stand for about 2 minutes until softened. Drain. Cover to keep warm.

Stir soy sauce into cornstarch in small bowl. Add next 3 ingredients. Stir. Set aside.

Heat wok or large frying pan on medium-high until very hot. Add cooking oil. Add next 4 ingredients. Stir-fry for 30 seconds.

(continued on next page)

Add onion and carrot. Stir-fry for 3 to 4 minutes until carrot is tender-crisp. Stir cornstarch mixture. Add to pork mixture. Heat and stir until boiling and thickened.

Divide and arrange next 4 ingredients among 4 large individual serving bowls. Cover with vermicelli. Spoon pork mixture over top.

Sprinkle individual servings with green onion and peanuts. Serves 4.

1 serving: 611 Calories; 27.2 g Total Fat (13.2 g Mono, 5.2 g Poly, 6.6 g Sat); 50 mg Cholesterol; 62 g Carbohydrate; 3 g Fibre; 25 g Protein; 1429 mg Sodium

Pictured below.

You can't wear these exquisite jewels—but you can eat them! Make this brightly-coloured, tender-crisp stir-fry your family treasure. Best served over rice vermicelli.

about veggie cooking

Think making a stir-fry is as easy as throwing a bunch of veggies into a wok and adding some sauce? Not quite. Timing is very important. After all, who wants to dine on raw cauliflower and soggy bean sprouts? Different veggies cook at different rates, so it is important they be added to a stir-fry at different times. If you want to substitute some of your favourite veggies consider the following: carrots, onions, broccoli, celery, cauliflower and asparagus should be added first because they take the longest time. Bell peppers, zucchini, snow peas and sugar snap peas should follow. And the quickest cookers are things like bean sprouts, green onions and leafy greens like bok choy or Chinese cabbage.

Many Jewels Stir-Fry

Water	1/3 cup	75 mL
Oyster sauce	1/3 cup	75 mL
Soy sauce	1/4 cup	60 mL
Cornstarch	2 tbsp.	30 mL
Dry sherry	1 tbsp.	15 mL
Brown sugar, packed	2 tsp.	10 mL
Cooking oil	2 tbsp.	30 mL
Medium carrot, decoratively cut	1	1
Fresh small chili pepper, finely diced (see Tip, page 62)	1	1
Garlic cloves, minced (or 3/4 tsp., 4 mL, powder)	3	3
Finely grated gingerroot (or 1/4 – 3/4 tsp., 1 – 4 mL, ground ginger)	1 – 3 tsp.	5 – 15 mL
Small green pepper, cut into 3/4 inch (2 cm) diamond shapes	1	1
Small red pepper, cut into 3/4 inch (2 cm) diamond shapes	1	1
Small yellow pepper, cut into 3/4 inch (2 cm) diamond shapes	1	1
Medium zucchini, quartered lengthwise and cut into 1/2 inch (12 mm) pieces	1	1
Quartered fresh white mushrooms	1 1/2 cups	375 mL
Can of sliced water chestnuts, drained	8 oz.	227 mL
Sesame seeds, toasted (see Tip, page 56)	1 tbsp.	15 mL

Combine first 6 ingredients in small bowl. Set aside.

Heat wok or large frying pan on medium-high until very hot. Add cooking oil. Add next 4 ingredients. Stir-fry for about 1 minute until fragrant.

Add next 3 ingredients. Stir-fry for 2 minutes.

Add next 3 ingredients. Stir-fry for 2 to 3 minutes until zucchini is tender-crisp. Stir cornstarch mixture. Add to vegetable mixture. Heat and stir until sauce is boiling and thickened.

(continued on next page)

Sprinkle with sesame seeds. Serves 4.

1 serving: 184 Calories; 8.5 g Total Fat (4.6 g Mono, 2.8 g Poly, 0.7 g Sat); 0 mg Cholesterol;
24 g Carbohydrate; 3 g Fibre; 5 g Protein; 1479 mg Sodium

Pictured below.

Get keen on green bean cuisine! Crunchy almonds and crisp veggies combine in this enchantingly light stir-fry.

Green Bean Stir-Fry

Slivered almonds	1/4 cup	60 mL
Low-sodium soy sauce	1 tbsp.	15 mL
Salt	1/4 tsp.	1 mL
Garlic powder	1/4 tsp.	1 mL
Ground ginger	1/8 tsp.	0.5 mL
Cooking oil	1 tbsp.	15 mL
Frozen cut green beans	2 cups	500 mL
Sliced fresh white mushrooms	1 cup	250 mL
Frozen kernel corn	1 cup	250 mL
Green onions, sliced	4	4

Combine first 5 ingredients in small bowl. Set aside.

Heat wok or large frying pan on medium-high until very hot. Add cooking oil. Add green beans. Stir-fry for 4 minutes.

Add remaining 3 ingredients. Stir-fry for 2 minutes. Add almond mixture. Stir-fry until heated through. Serves 4.

1 serving: 138 Calories; 7.2 g Total Fat (4.3 g Mono, 2 g Poly, 0.6 g Sat); 0 mg Cholesterol; 16 g Carbohydrate; 4 g Fibre; 4 g Protein; 318 mg Sodium

A wholesome, healthy stir-fry that's also easy to make. These garden-fresh vegetables are tossed in a sauce that won't overpower your taste buds.

Chinese Stir-Fry Vegetables

Prepared chicken (or vegetable) broth	1/2 cup	125 mL
Cornstarch	1 tbsp.	15 mL
Soy sauce	2 tsp.	10 mL
Granulated sugar	1 1/2 tsp.	7 mL
Salt	1 tsp.	5 mL
Cooking oil	2 tbsp.	30 mL
Snow peas, trimmed	2 1/4 cups	550 mL
Sliced fresh white mushrooms	1 1/2 cups	375 mL
Small cauliflower florets	3/4 cup	175 mL
Small broccoli florets	3/4 cup	175 mL
Thinly sliced carrot	3/4 cup	175 mL
Thinly sliced celery	1/3 cup	75 mL
Thinly sliced green onion	1/3 cup	75 mL

(continued on next page)

Stir broth into cornstarch in small bowl. Add next 3 ingredients. Stir. Set aside.

Heat wok or large frying pan on medium-high until very hot. Add cooking oil. Add remaining 7 ingredients. Stir-fry for 3 to 5 minutes until vegetables are tender-crisp. Stir cornstarch mixture. Add to vegetable mixture. Heat and stir for about 2 minutes until boiling and thickened. Serves 4.

1 serving: 144 Calories; 7.4 g Total Fat (4.1 g Mono, 2.2 g Poly, 0.6 g Sat); 0 mg Cholesterol; 16 g Carbohydrate; 4 g Fibre; 5 g Protein; 942 mg Sodium

Pictured below.

Can vegetables be an indulgence? You bet! With a creamy, yet light, cheese sauce, vegetables can be downright decadent! An excellent choice for a dinner party.

about cutting veggies

Stir-fries are a bit paradoxical in nature—they cook really fast but their prep may take quite a while. The reason a stir-fry cooks so quickly is because the ingredients used are cut into small, similar-sized pieces. Which is also the reason the prep takes so long—you have to cut things into small, similar-sized pieces! This is important, not only because it speeds up cooking time but, because if the pieces are all the same size, they all get cooked to the same doneness. So what is a person without cutting skills of lightning speed supposed to do? Invest in a mandolin-type slicer which cuts vegetables uniformly, buy pre-cut veggies or practice, practice, practice!

Pasta Primavera

Spaghetti, broken into thirds	8 oz.	225 g
Cooking oil	1 tsp.	5 mL
Can of skim evaporated milk	13 1/2 oz.	385 mL
Grated Parmesan cheese	2/3 cup	150 mL
Chopped fresh parsley (or 1 tbsp., 15 mL, flakes)	1/4 cup	60 mL
Chopped fresh basil (or 1 tbsp., 15 mL, dried)	1/4 cup	60 mL
Salt	1 tsp.	5 mL
Pepper	1/4 tsp.	1 mL
Cooking oil	2 tsp.	15 mL
Medium carrots, julienned (see Tip, page 110)	2	2
Medium onion, thinly sliced	1	1
Thinly sliced celery	1/2 cup	125 mL
Garlic clove, minced (or 1/4 tsp., 1 mL, powder)	1	1
Cooking oil	1 tbsp.	15 mL
Small cauliflower florets	1 cup	250 mL
Small broccoli florets	1 cup	250 mL
Box of frozen snow peas, partially thawed (or 2 cups, 500 mL, fresh)	6 oz.	170 g
Julienned zucchini (see Tip, page 110)	1 cup	250 mL
Cherry tomatoes, halved	8	8
Grated Parmesan cheese, sprinkle		

Cook spaghetti in boiling salted water in large uncovered saucepan or Dutch oven for about 10 minutes, stirring occasionally, until tender but firm. Drain. Return to same pot.

Add first amount of cooking oil. Toss. Cover to keep warm.

Combine next 6 ingredients in small bowl. Set aside.

Heat wok or large frying pan on medium-high until very hot. Add second amount of cooking oil. Add next 4 ingredients. Stir-fry for about 2 minutes until tender-crisp. Transfer to separate small bowl. Cover to keep warm.

(continued on next page)

Add third amount of cooking oil to hot wok. Add cauliflower and broccoli. Stir-fry for about 4 minutes until almost cooked.

Add snow peas and zucchini. Stir-fry for 2 to 3 minutes until tender-crisp. Add carrot mixture.

Add tomato and milk mixture. Stir-fry until heated through. Add spaghetti. Stir.

Sprinkle with Parmesan cheese. Serves 4.

1 serving: 507 Calories; 13.8 g Total Fat (5.8 g Mono, 2.9 g Poly, 4.1 g Sat); 16 mg Cholesterol; 70 g Carbohydrate; 8 g Fibre; 27 g Protein; 1067 mg Sodium

Pictured below.

A simply hoi-sinful mix of tender-crisp vegetables and crunchy cashews! Serve with thick Shanghai noodles or steamed jasmine rice.

tip

To julienne vegetables, cut into 1/8 inch (3 mm) strips that resemble matchsticks.

Cashew Vegetable Stir-Fry

Water	1 tbsp.	15 mL
Cornstarch	2 tsp.	10 mL
Chinese dried mushrooms	12	12
Boiling water	1 cup	250 mL
Cooking oil	2 tsp.	10 mL
Large onion, cut into thin wedges	1	1
Fresh hot chili pepper, finely chopped (see Tip, page 62)	1	1
Garlic cloves, minced (or 1/2 tsp., 2 mL, powder)	2	2
Finely grated gingerroot (or 1/8 tsp., 0.5 mL, ground ginger)	1/2 tsp.	2 mL
Snow peas, trimmed	2 cups	500 mL
Medium red peppers, cut into thin strips	2	2
Green onions, cut into 1 inch (2.5 cm) pieces	12	12
Medium carrot, julienned (see Tip)	1	1
Oyster sauce	2 tbsp.	30 mL
Hoisin sauce	2 tbsp.	30 mL
Liquid honey	1 tbsp.	15 mL
Plain cashews	1/3 cup	75 mL
Finely shredded fresh basil	2 tbsp.	30 mL

Stir water into cornstarch in small cup. Set aside.

Put mushrooms into small heatproof bowl. Add boiling water. Stir. Let stand for about 20 minutes until softened. Drain. Remove and discard stems. Slice thinly. Set aside.

Heat wok or large frying pan on medium-high until very hot. Add cooking oil. Add next 4 ingredients. Stir-fry for about 2 minutes until fragrant.

Add next 4 ingredients. Stir-fry for 2 minutes.

Combine next 3 ingredients in separate small cup. Add to vegetable mixture. Add sliced mushrooms. Stir-fry for 2 to 3 minutes until vegetables are tender-crisp. Stir cornstarch mixture. Add to vegetable mixture. Heat and stir for about 1 minute until boiling and thickened.

(continued on next page)

Add cashews and basil. Toss. Serves 6.

1 serving: 153 Calories; 5.5 g Total Fat (3.0 g Mono, 1.3 g Poly, 0.9 g Sat); trace Cholesterol;
23 g Carbohydrate; 4 g Fibre; 4 g Protein; 148 mg Sodium

Pictured below and on back cover.

For those that like it hot, try adding more chili paste to this mild-flavoured noodle dish.

tip

Have your noodles got you in a sticky situation? After draining, rinse with cold water and toss with a very small amount of sesame oil. Your noodles will be tangle-free in no time!

Diced Tofu And Noodles

Apple juice	3/4 cup	175 mL
Apple cider vinegar	1 tbsp.	15 mL
Soy sauce	1 tbsp.	15 mL
Garlic clove, minced (or 1/4 tsp., 1 mL, powder)	1	1
Chili paste (sambal oelek)	1/2 tsp.	2 mL
Package of extra-firm tofu, cut into 1/2 inch (12 mm) cubes	12 1/4 oz.	350 g
Cornstarch	1 tbsp.	15 mL
Dry, thin Chinese-style instant noodles	7 oz.	200 g
Sesame (or cooking) oil	1 tsp.	5 mL
Cooking oil	2 tbsp.	30 mL
Can of cut baby corn, drained	14 oz	398 mL
Sliced fresh white mushrooms	1 cup	250 mL
Chopped onion	1 cup	250 mL
Diced green pepper	1/2 cup	125 mL
Diced red pepper	1/2 cup	125 mL
Salt, sprinkle		
Pepper, sprinkle		

Combine first 5 ingredients in medium bowl.

Add tofu. Stir gently. Let stand at room temperature for 1 hour, stirring gently once or twice. Remove tofu to plate using slotted spoon. Set aside.

Stir cornstarch into apple juice mixture. Set aside.

Cook noodles in boiling salted water in large uncovered saucepan or Dutch oven for 4 to 6 minutes, stirring occasionally, until tender but firm. Drain. Return to same pot. Add sesame oil. Toss. Cover to keep warm.

Heat wok or large frying pan on medium-high until very hot. Add cooking oil. Add remaining 7 ingredients. Stir-fry for about 2 minutes until vegetables are tender-crisp. Stir cornstarch mixture. Add to vegetable mixture. Heat and stir until boiling and thickened. Add tofu. Stir gently until heated through. Arrange noodles on platter. Top with tofu mixture. Serves 4.

1 serving: 530 Calories; 11.2 g Total Fat (5.1 g Mono, 4.1 g Poly, 1.2 g Sat); 0 mg Cholesterol; 95 g Carbohydrate; 5 g Fibre; 18 g Protein; 617 mg Sodium

Pictured at right.

Think tofu's bland? Not when it's coated with a sweet teriyaki glaze. And to please you even further, dinner will be on the table chop-chop!

serving suggestion

Make Chop-Chop Teriyaki Tofu a meal by serving it over fried mushrooms and Chinese-style egg noodles. First, cook the noodles according to package directions, drain, then fry with small pieces of brown mushrooms in a small amount of oil.

Chop-Chop Teriyaki Tofu

Thick teriyaki basting sauce	1/2 cup	125 mL
Brown sugar, packed	1 tsp.	5 mL
Package of firm tofu, diced	12 1/4 oz.	350 g
Water	1 tbsp.	15 mL
Cornstarch	2 tsp.	10 mL
Cooking oil	2 tsp.	10 mL
Chopped onion	1/2 cup	125 mL
Garlic clove, minced (or 1/4 tsp., 1 mL, powder)	1	1
Finely grated gingerroot (or 1/4 tsp., 1 mL, ground ginger)	1 tsp.	5 mL
Frozen California mixed vegetables, thawed	2 cups	500 mL
Chopped fresh cilantro or parsley (optional)	1 tbsp.	15 mL

Combine teriyaki sauce and brown sugar in medium bowl.

Add tofu. Stir gently. Cover. Let stand in refrigerator for at least 10 minutes.

Stir water into cornstarch in small cup. Set aside.

Heat wok or large frying pan on medium-high until very hot. Add cooking oil. Add next 3 ingredients. Stir-fry for 2 to 3 minutes until onion starts to soften.

Add vegetables. Stir-fry for 2 to 3 minutes until onion is softened. Add tofu mixture. Stir gently. Stir cornstarch mixture. Add to tofu mixture. Reduce heat to low. Heat and stir for 3 to 4 minutes until tofu is heated through and sauce is boiling and thickened.

Sprinkle with cilantro. Serves 4.

1 serving: 163 Calories; 4.7 g Total Fat (1.8 g Mono, 2.0 g Poly, 0.5 g Sat); 0 mg Cholesterol; 22 g Carbohydrate; 2 g Fibre; 9 g Protein; 862 mg Sodium

Pictured at right.

Top: Stir-Fried Honey Greens, page 116
Bottom: Chop-Chop Teriyaki Tofu, above

Know someone whose sweet tooth makes them finicky when it comes to eating veggies? Well, converting them will be like taking candy from them, baby! (And giving them something much healthier to eat.)

Stir-Fried Honey Greens

Hoisin sauce	1 tbsp.	15 mL
Cornstarch	2 tsp.	10 mL
Liquid honey	1 tbsp.	15 mL
Cooking oil	1 tsp.	5 mL
Chopped bok choy	3 cups	750 mL
Fresh asparagus, trimmed of tough ends and cut into 2 inch (5 cm) pieces	1 lb.	454 g

Stir hoisin sauce into cornstarch in small cup. Add honey. Stir.

Heat wok or large frying pan on medium-high until very hot. Add cooking oil. Add bok choy and asparagus. Stir-fry for 4 to 5 minutes until vegetables are tender-crisp. Stir cornstarch mixture. Add to vegetable mixture. Stir-fry for about 1 minute until boiling and thickened. Serves 6.

1 serving: 49 Calories; 1.1 g Total Fat (0.5 g Mono, 0.4 g Poly, 0.1 g Sat); trace Cholesterol; 9 g Carbohydrate; 2 g Fibre; 2.3 g Protein; 67 mg Sodium

Pictured on page 115.

This braise is sure to amaze! We've raided the vegetable garden to give you a medley of some of the most loved Asian veggies—all in one dish! Adjust the amount of chili paste to suit your preference.

tip

If a recipe calls for Shanghai bok choy and it is not available, substitute baby bok choy.

Braised Vegetables

Chinese dried mushrooms	6	6
Boiling water	1 cup	250 mL
Prepared vegetable broth	1/4 cup	60 mL
Low-sodium soy sauce	1 tbsp.	15 mL
Hoisin sauce	1 tbsp.	15 mL
Chili paste (sambal oelek)	1 tsp.	5 mL
Water	1 tbsp.	15 mL
Cornstarch	2 tsp.	10 mL
Peanut (or cooking) oil	1 tbsp.	15 mL
Heads of Shanghai bok choy, trimmed and separated into leaves (see Tip)	3	3
Whole baby bok choy, trimmed and separated into leaves	2	2
Can of sliced water chestnuts, drained	8 oz.	227 mL
Green onions, cut into 1 inch (2.5 cm) pieces	8	8

(continued on next page)

Put mushrooms into small heatproof bowl. Add boiling water. Stir. Let stand for about 20 minutes until softened. Drain. Remove and discard stems. Slice thinly. Set aside.

Combine next 4 ingredients in separate small bowl. Set aside.

Stir water into cornstarch in small cup.

Heat wok or large frying pan on medium-high until very hot. Add peanut oil. Add next 4 ingredients and sliced mushrooms. Stir-fry for 1 minute. Stir broth mixture. Add to vegetable mixture. Stir-fry for about 3 minutes until vegetables are tender-crisp. Stir cornstarch mixture. Add to vegetable mixture. Heat and stir until boiling and thickened. Serves 4.

1 serving: 118 Calories; 4.0 g Total Fat (1.6 g Mono, 1.4 g Poly, 0.6 g Sat); trace Cholesterol; 18 g Carbohydrate; 4 g Fibre; 4 g Protein; 352 mg Sodium

Pictured below.

Don't carrot all for veggies? This speedy side dish coated with crunchy almonds and sweetened with a touch of honey is sure to change your mind! An excellent side for a seafood dish.

about couscous

Conjuring up visions of Casablanca, this North African staple is most commonly made from semolina—the same wheat product used to make pasta. More and more in North America, it's becoming a great friend to the economy-minded and time-crunched cook because it is relatively inexpensive and can be prepared in 5 minutes (though if you're making it by hand, be prepared to spend several hours tending to it!). The perfect couscous will be moist and tender but never dry, wet or mushy.

Vegetable Couscous

Prepared chicken (or vegetable) broth	1 cup	250 mL
Couscous	1 cup	250 mL
Olive (or cooking) oil	2 tsp.	10 mL
Slivered almonds, toasted (see Tip, page 56)	1/4 cup	60 mL
Liquid honey	1 tbsp.	15 mL
Parsley flakes	2 tsp.	10 mL
Olive (or cooking) oil	1 tbsp.	15 mL
Thinly sliced carrot	1/2 cup	125 mL
Chopped zucchini	2 cups	500 mL
Sliced green onion	1/2 cup	125 mL
Frozen peas	1/2 cup	125 mL
Salt	1/2 tsp.	2 mL

Measure broth into medium saucepan. Bring to a boil. Remove from heat. Add couscous and first amount of olive oil. Stir. Cover. Let stand for 5 minutes. Fluff with fork.

Add next 3 ingredients. Stir well. Cover to keep warm.

Heat large frying pan or wok on medium-high until very hot. Add second amount of olive oil. Add carrot. Stir-fry for about 4 minutes until starting to brown.

Add remaining 4 ingredients. Stir-fry for about 4 minutes until zucchini is tender-crisp. Add couscous mixture. Toss well. Serves 4.

1 serving: 322 Calories; 9.9 g Total Fat (6.5 g Mono, 1.6 g Poly, 1.2 g Sat); 0 mg Cholesterol; 48 g Carbohydrate; 5 g Fibre; 10 g Protein; 532 mg Sodium

Pictured at right.

Top: Sesame Snow Peas, page 120
Bottom: Vegetable Couscous, above

These peas are sure to please. If snow peas are your favourite part of a stir-fry, you'll love this dish that's nothing but!

Sesame Snow Peas

Cooking oil	2 tsp.	10 mL
Chopped green onion	1/2 cup	125 mL
Rice vinegar	1 tbsp.	15 mL
Granulated sugar	2 tsp.	10 mL
Hoisin sauce	2 tsp.	10 mL
Sesame oil	1 tsp.	5 mL
Snow peas, trimmed	3 cups	750 mL
Sesame seeds, toasted (see Tip, page 56)	2 tbsp.	30 mL
Lemon juice	1 tbsp.	15 mL

Heat large frying pan or wok on medium-high until very hot. Add cooking oil. Add next 5 ingredients. Heat and stir for about 1 minute until sugar is dissolved.

Add snow peas. Cook for about 3 minutes, stirring often, until tender-crisp.

Add sesame seeds and lemon juice. Stir. Serves 4.

1 serving: 112 Calories; 5.9 g Total Fat (2.7 g Mono, 2.3 g Poly, 0.7 g Sat); trace Cholesterol; 12 g Carbohydrate; 3 g Fibre; 3 g Protein; 53 mg Sodium

Pictured on page 119.

Colourful and tasty. With few ingredients and minimal prep time— this dish is nothing short of superb!

Bean Sprouts And Peppers

Cooking oil	2 tsp.	10 mL
Medium green pepper, sliced	1	1
Medium red pepper, sliced	1	1
Finely grated gingerroot (or 1/4 tsp., 1 mL, ground ginger)	1 tsp.	5 mL
Salt	1/2 tsp.	2 mL
Fresh bean sprouts	1 1/2 cups	375 mL
Chicken (or vegetable) bouillon powder	1 tsp.	5 mL
Hot water	1/4 cup	60 mL

Heat wok or large frying pan on medium-high until very hot. Add cooking oil. Add next 4 ingredients. Stir-fry for 2 minutes.

(continued on next page)

Add bean sprouts. Stir-fry for 1 minute.

Stir bouillon powder into hot water in small cup. Add to vegetable mixture. Cook, covered, for 2 to 3 minutes until boiling. Serves 4.

1 serving: *47 Calories; 2.5 g Total Fat (1.4 g Mono, 0.8 g Poly, 0.2 g Sat); 0 mg Cholesterol; 6 g Carbohydrate; 1.8 g Fibre; 2 g Protein; 524 mg Sodium*

Pictured below.

We're not trying to shanghai you, these easy noodles will take your taste buds on a tantalizing flavour adventure. Great served with chicken or on their own.

food fun

So you're cooking up a big pot of stew, and forks and spoons haven't been invented yet. How would you retrieve your food without burning your fingers? You might just grab a couple of sticks from the nearest tree and dig in. According to scientists, that's probably how chopsticks were invented in China about 5000 years ago. Supposedly, Confucius was a big fan of chopsticks—he believed that knives, which were associated with violence, had no place at the dining table. By about 500 AD, chopsticks had spread to many parts of Asia, where they found many uses—in religious ceremonies, as fireplace tongs, and even as martial arts weapons! But today, we're happy to say, they're most popular as eating utensils.

Shanghai Noodles

Fresh, thin Chinese-style egg noodles	12 oz.	340 g
Peanut (or cooking) oil	1 tbsp.	15 mL
Medium onion, cut into thin wedges	1	1
Chopped red pepper	1 cup	250 mL
Chopped green onion	1/2 cup	125 mL
Chinese satay sauce	1/4 cup	60 mL
Prepared chicken (or vegetable) broth	1/4 cup	60 mL
Soy sauce	2 tbsp.	30 mL
Sesame oil (optional)	2 tsp.	10 mL

Put noodles into large heatproof bowl. Cover with boiling water. Let stand for about 5 minutes until softened. Drain. Cover to keep warm.

Heat wok or large frying pan on medium-high until very hot. Add peanut oil. Add next 4 ingredients. Stir-fry for about 1 minute until fragrant.

Add noodles and remaining 3 ingredients. Stir-fry for 3 to 5 minutes until onion is tender-crisp. Serves 6.

1 serving: 225 Calories; 4.4 g Total Fat (1.1 g Mono, 0.8 g Poly, 1.6 g Sat); 5 mg Cholesterol; 39 g Carbohydrate; 3 g Fibre; 9 g Protein; 664 mg Sodium

Pictured at right.

Throughout this book measurements are given in Conventional and Metric measure. To compensate for differences between the two measurements due to rounding, a full metric measure is not always used. The cup used is the standard 8 fluid ounce. Temperature is given in degrees Fahrenheit and Celsius. Baking pan measurements are in inches and centimetres as well as quarts and litres. An exact metric conversion is given on this page as well as the working equivalent (Metric Standard Measure).

Pans

Conventional – Inches	Metric – Centimetres
8 × 8 inch	20 × 20 cm
9 × 9 inch	22 × 22 cm
9 × 13 inch	22 × 33 cm
10 × 15 inch	25 × 38 cm
11 × 17 inch	28 × 43 cm
8 × 2 inch round	20 × 5 cm
9 × 2 inch round	22 × 5 cm
10 × 4 1/2 inch tube	25 × 11 cm
8 × 4 × 3 inch loaf	20 × 10 × 7.5 cm
9 × 5 × 3 inch loaf	22 × 12.5 × 7.5 cm

Oven Temperatures

Fahrenheit (°F)	Celsius (°C)	Fahrenheit (°F)	Celsius (°C)
175°	80°	350°	175°
200°	95°	375°	190°
225°	110°	400°	205°
250°	120°	425°	220°
275°	140°	450°	230°
300°	150°	475°	240°
325°	160°	500°	260°

Spoons

Conventional Measure	Metric Exact Conversion Millilitre (mL)	Metric Standard Measure Millilitre (mL)
1/8 teaspoon (tsp.)	0.6 mL	0.5 mL
1/4 teaspoon (tsp.)	1.2 mL	1 mL
1/2 teaspoon (tsp.)	2.4 mL	2 mL
1 teaspoon (tsp.)	4.7 mL	5 mL
2 teaspoons (tsp.)	9.4 mL	10 mL
1 tablespoon (tbsp.)	14.2 mL	15 mL

Cups

1/4 cup (4 tbsp.)	56.8 mL	60 mL
1/3 cup (5 1/3 tbsp.)	75.6 mL	75 mL
1/2 cup (8 tbsp.)	113.7 mL	125 mL
2/3 cup (10 2/3 tbsp.)	151.2 mL	150 mL
3/4 cup (12 tbsp.)	170.5 mL	175 mL
1 cup (16 tbsp.)	227.3 mL	250 mL
4 1/2 cups	1022.9 mL	1000 mL (1 L)

Dry Measurements

Conventional Measure Ounces (oz.)	Metric Exact Conversion Grams (g)	Metric Standard Measure Grams (g)
1 oz.	28.3 g	28 g
2 oz.	56.7 g	57 g
3 oz.	85.0 g	85 g
4 oz.	113.4 g	125 g
5 oz.	141.7 g	140 g
6 oz.	170.1 g	170 g
7 oz.	198.4 g	200 g
8 oz.	226.8 g	250 g
16 oz.	453.6 g	500 g
32 oz.	907.2 g	1000 g (1 kg)

Casseroles

Canada & Britain		United States	
Standard Size Casserole	Exact Metric Measure	Standard Size Casserole	Exact Metric Measure
1 qt. (5 cups)	1.13 L	1 qt. (4 cups)	900 mL
1 1/2 qts. (7 1/2 cups)	1.69 L	1 1/2 qts. (6 cups)	1.35 L
2 qts. (10 cups)	2.25 L	2 qts. (8 cups)	1.8 L
2 1/2 qts. (12 1/2 cups)	2.81 L	2 1/2 qts. (10 cups)	2.25 L
3 qts. (15 cups)	3.38 L	3 qts. (12 cups)	2.7 L
4 qts. (20 cups)	4.5 L	4 qts. (16 cups)	3.6 L
5 qts. (25 cups)	5.63 L	5 qts. (20 cups)	4.5 L

Tip Index

Recipe Index

most loved recipe collection most loved recipe collection